Broadcast:
ABC
WORLD NEWS TONIGHT

3

Shigeru Yamane
Kathleen Yamane

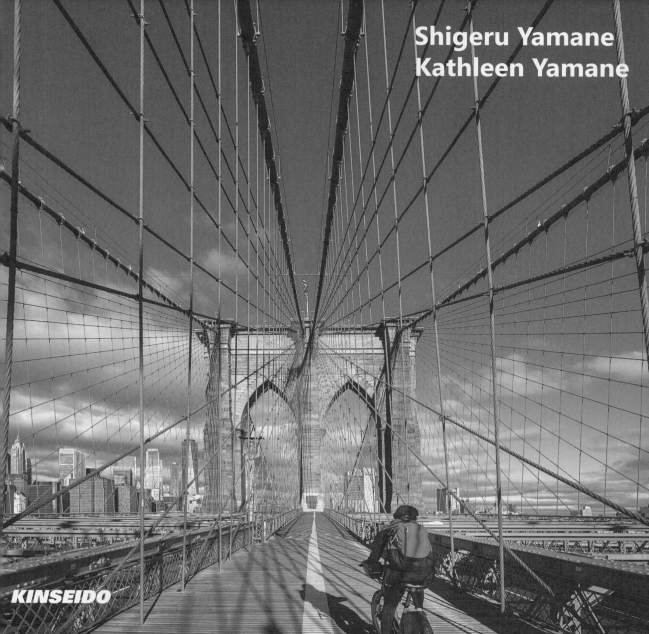

KINSEIDO

Kinseido Publishing Co., Ltd.
3-21 Kanda Jimbo-cho, Chiyoda-ku,
Tokyo 101-0051, Japan

First published 2021 by Kinseido Publishing Co., Ltd.

Foreword

World News Tonight, the flagship news program of the American Broadcast Company, is enjoyed by millions of Americans each evening at 6:30. With its reputation for balanced, fair reporting by a news team who take a personalized look at what's happening around the world and report it with heart, the show is consistently at the top of the evening news ratings.

Since the publication of this textbook series began more than three decades ago, the popular newscasts have become part of the learning experience of thousands of Japanese students, as well. This text is the third in our new series, incorporating several changes that we feel enhance the learning experience. As always, we have made every effort to select stories that are not only important but will also make young adults think a little bit harder about the world outside of Japan. This book includes a stimulating cross section of topics, from the history of authentic "Made-in-America" cowboy hats to the current laws on vaping. Students will meet heroes like Katherine Johnson, who broke racial and gender barriers in her work for NASA's moon flights, and American volunteers helping their neighbors during the pandemic. The stories will take you all across the U.S. and beyond, introducing you to indigenous tribesmen fighting to protect the Amazon rainforest and residents of Venice, anxious about the flooding in their iconic city. We feel certain that you will find them all to be as fascinating as we do.

Back in 1987, no one associated with this ABC World News textbook project imagined that the series would have such longevity and touch the lives of so many students. We believe that adopting authentic broadcast news materials for classroom use is a powerful way to build English skills while also helping students to become more knowledgeable about world affairs and to develop the critical thinking skills necessary for all young people in today's increasingly interconnected world. Many of our students also tell us that using the text was good preparation for the TOEFL and TOEIC exams and for job interviews.

To the students using *Broadcast: ABC WORLD NEWS TONIGHT 3*, remember that the skills that you develop using this book can be applied to other news shows, even when the course is over. We sincerely hope that you will challenge yourselves to become more aware of world events and be inspired to follow the news more closely. Happy studying!

January 2021

Kathleen Yamane

Shigeru Yamane

まえがき

近年，日常生活における情報源としてインターネットの活用がますます盛んになってきている。このような高度な情報化社会では，不正確な情報や見方の偏った情報も多くあふれている。学生諸君は，何が本当に自分に役立つ正しい情報か，情報の「質」を見極める能力を身につける必要があるのではないだろうか。

一般的に，テレビニュースからの情報は信頼性が高いといわれている。本書はアメリカの３大ネットワーク（ABC，CBS，NBC）の一つである，ABC放送からのテレビニュース番組を録画し，それを文字化した上で，テキスト用に編集したものである。収録したニュースはアメリカ東部標準時間夕方6時30分から毎日放送されているABC放送の看板ニュース番組*ABC World News Tonight*である。

1948年に始まり，長い歴史を誇るこのABC放送のニュース番組は，ピーター・ジェニングズなど，多くの人気キャスターを生み出してきた。2014年にディビッド・ミュアがアンカーパーソンに抜擢され，さらに人気が高まった。2015年３月には「アメリカで最も多く視聴されている夕方のニュース番組」となり，アメリカ国内でも絶大な人気を保ちながら，質の高い情報を毎日提供し続けている。

今回も，そのABC放送の看板番組の中から，大学生が学ぶにふさわしい多種多様なニュースを15本厳選し，収録することができた。アメリカ国内のニュースだけではなく，「ベネチア水没の危機」や「アマゾンの熱帯雨林を守る先住民族」など，世界のニュースも含まれている。さらに，「苦闘する中小企業の経営者」，「人種差別に対する抗議デモが全米で広がる」など，本書で取り上げた現代社会が抱えるさまざまなトピックを学ぶことを通じて，学生諸君にはニュースの理解を深めながら，自分の意見も持ってもらいたい。また，身近で親しみやすい話題としては，「退役軍人の手作りのおもちゃ」，考えさせる話題としては，「特別支援が必要な人を雇用する」など多く収録した。

ニュースを収録した映像は、専用のウェブサイトplus+Media上でストリーミング視聴することができる。ぜひ，学生諸君にはこの映像を繰り返し見てもらいたい。アメリカの家庭で毎日アメリカ人が見ている良質のニュース番組に触れ，信頼できる情報をもとに英語を学んでもらいたい。

本書は1987年に*TV News from the U.S.A.*として始まった。その後，1999年から*ABC World News*として20年間毎年出版され続けた。また2019年には，さまざまな箇所に改良を加え，*Broadcast: ABC WORLD NEWS TONIGHT*と書名を変更し生まれ変わった。アメリカABC放送のニュースを利用した本シリーズは，今回で通算28冊目になり，お陰様で毎回たいへん好評を頂いている。2010年度には外国語教育メディア学会（LET）から，本教材の開発に対して，LET学会賞の「教材開発賞」を受賞する栄誉を頂いた。今後もさらにより良い教材開発の努力を続けていきたい。

最後になったが，テキスト作成に際して毎回大変お世話になっている金星堂のみなさん，今回もこころよく版権を許可してくださったアメリカABC放送に心から感謝の意を表したい。

2021年1月

山根　繁

Kathleen Yamane

abc NEWS

Broadcast: ABC WORLD NEWS TONIGHT

3

Table of Contents

Appendix
   Map of the United States
   TVニュース英語とは
   最近のTVニュースに現れた略語

News Story 1

New Company

Before	You Watch the News

Preview Questions

1. What has become a popular way for many Americans to seek comfort during the pandemic?
   ——パンデミックの間，多くのアメリカ人にとって癒しを求めるために人気になった方法とは何ですか。

2. What are some people saying about the trend?
   ——そのトレンドについて，人はどのように言っていますか。

Warm-up Exercises

A Vocabulary Check: Choose the correct definition for each of the words below.

1. companion ( )
2. foster ( )
3. cuddle ( )
4. ache ( )
5. handful ( )

a. to suffer from pain
b. to hold close in one's arms; to hug
c. a person or animal with whom one spends time
d. to bring up or care for a child or animal that is not one's own
e. someone who is troublesome or difficult to control

B Fill in the blanks with appropriate expressions from the Vocabulary Check above. Change the word forms where necessary.

1. Meg and Mia took turns (   ) their new baby brother.
2. My brother's three kids are cute, but they can be a real (   ).
3. Grandma is looking for a traveling (   ) for her trip to France.
4. Your foot is still (   )? You should see a doctor.
5. They have two sons of their own, and have decided to (   ) a little girl.

News Story [1' 53"]

T. Llamas: Finally tonight, the new companions bringing some much-needed comfort to families all across the country.

You're watching workers at the Palm Beach County Animal Care and Control Shelter cheering because for the first time ever, going all the way back to 1969, an entire section of dog kennels is empty. Some positive rays breaking through all those coronavirus clouds. Pet adoptions are soaring. Around the country, happy dogs. And their new owners, getting to know each other. In Plano, Texas, the Cabesa family with three-month-old Coco, **1.** _____

_____.

Pet owner 1: We thought that during the stay-at-home requirements, it was a good time to help her become a good member of our family.

T. Llamas: UPenn senior Alexandra Sharp from central Michigan fostering one-year-old Opal. She decided to foster during this global pandemic to give dogs **2.** _____

_____.

Pet owner 2: I've really loved having Opal. She's so sweet, so cute, so fun. Ah... I feel like she brings a lot of joy to the house during a time, you know, that's really difficult for everyone. So, um, fostering has been awesome, and honestly now I think I want to adopt her.

T. Llamas: In Milwaukee, Emmy 3. _____,

the Luomas. The Wisconsin Humane Society telling us today, 580 of their animals have been adopted since March, including these three lab mix puppies.

Pet owner 3: Good morning.

T. Llamas: They just got adopted by three thrilled families. Just look at Kevin today with his new owners. While his brother, Duncan, cuddling up with the Gilbert family. For so many aching hearts, 4. _____ _____, four legs and endless energy, the perfect prescription.

Duncan looks like a handful. Enjoy those new pups. We thank those families for talking to us tonight and 5. _____ _____. I'm Tom Llamas in New York. Please stay safe. Good night.

Notes **Palm Beach County Animal Care and Control Shelter**「パームビーチ郡動物保護管理シェルター〈パームビーチ郡は，フロリダ半島の南東部，大西洋岸に位置する郡〉」 **Pet adoptions**「ペットの里親になること；ペットを正式に引き取ること」 **Plano**「プレイノ〈テキサス州北部の都市〉」 **UPenn senior**「ペンシルベニア大学４年生〈UPenn=The University of Pennsylvania〉」 **global pandemic**「世界的なパンデミック；世界中にまん延している感染症〈新型コロナウイルス〉」 **awesome**「素晴らしい；すごい；最高の」 **adopt**「里親になる〈foster は，ペットを（里親が見つかるまで）一時的にボランティアに預かってもらうことで，adopt は，正式に譲渡してもらって里親となることを意味する〉」 **Milwaukee**「ミルウォーキー〈ウィスコンシン州南東部，ミシガン湖に臨む都市〉」 **Wisconsin Humane Society**「ウィスコンシン州動物愛護協会」 **lab mix**「ラブラドール・レトリバーの雑種〈lab mix= Labrador retriever mix〉」 **thrilled**「大喜びしている」 **prescription**「（心を癒やす）処方薬」 **pups**「子犬〈pups= puppies〉」

After You Watch the News

Exercises
A Listen to the CD and fill in the blanks in the text.

◎ CD 02

B Multiple Choice Questions

1. According to the news story
   a. a record number of dogs are being adopted.
   b. more people are fostering rather than adopting dogs.
   c. there are not enough dogs for all the people who want to adopt a pet.

2. Which is *NOT* cited as a reason for more dogs being adopted?
   a. People want to share the joy that they are feeling.
   b. People can't go out, so they are spending more time at home.
   c. People are going through difficult times and feel sad.

3. Opal
   a. is described as being a handful.
   b. is being fostered but will not be adopted.
   c. is a good companion for a university student.

4. Kevin and Duncan
   a. are two brothers who are thrilled with their new pet.
   b. are lab puppies from the Palm Beach County Animal Care and Control Shelter.
   c. are among the 580 dogs adopted from the Wisconsin Humane Society since March.

C Translate the following Japanese into English. Then listen to the CD and practice the conversation with your partner. ⊙ CD 03

A: Hey, don't you have to go to work today?

B: Nope! ¹._____

_____. I have nothing to do.

A: Empty? What do you mean? Did the dogs all run away?

B: No! ²._____.

A: But there were hundreds of dogs there just a few months ago.

B: It's incredible, isn't it? ³._____.

A: Why don't we adopt a dog?

B: I was thinking the same thing!

1. 犬小屋は 50 年ぶりに空っぽになりました。

2. みんな里親が見つかったのですよ。

3. 人々は今，良い仲間を必要としているのです。

D **Summary Practice: Fill in the blanks with suitable words beginning with the letters indicated.**

⊙ CD 04

ABC News reports on one popular way many Americans are seeking
(¹· **c**   ) during the pandemic: (²· **p**   ) (³· **a**   ).
Described as a (⁴· **p**   ) ray breaking through the
(⁵· **c**   ) (⁶· **c**   ), the (⁷· **s**   ) rate
of adoptions is good news for the dogs as well as their new (⁸· **o**   ).
Workers at the Palm Beach County (⁹· **A**   ) (¹⁰· **C**   ) and
Control Shelter are thrilled that for the first time since 1969, a whole
(¹¹· **s**   ) of their (¹²· **k**   ) is (¹³· **e**   ). Why
the big change? The Cabesa family of Texas felt that the (¹⁴· **s**   )-at-
(¹⁵· **h**   ) (¹⁶· **r**   ) made it a perfect time for their new
pet Coco to become a good (¹⁷· **m**   ) of the (¹⁸· **f**   ).
Across the country, for families like the Luomas and the Gilberts,
(¹⁹· **c**   ) their new pets is the perfect (²⁰· **m**   )
during this difficult time.

E **Discussion: Share your ideas and opinions with your classmates.**

1. According to the news story, pet adoptions are one way that Americans
have found comfort during the pandemic. Have pet adoptions increased
in Japan during the pandemic?

2. What are other ways that people have sought comfort during the
pandemic when they cannot go out or meet their friends? What do you
do?

3. There are many famous sayings about the special relationship between
humans and dogs, such as "Happiness is a warm puppy" and "A dog is
the only thing on earth that loves you more than he loves himself." Do
you know of any other sayings about dogs?

News Story 2

E-Cigarette: Partial Ban Backlash

Air Date: January 2, 2020
Duration: 1′ 55″

Preview Questions

1. Why are e-cigarettes being banned?
——なぜ電子たばこは禁止されているのですか。

2. What is President Trump's position on the issue?
——この件について，トランプ大統領はどのような立場をとっていますか。

Warm-up Exercises

A **Vocabulary Check: Choose the correct definition for each of the words below.**

1. restriction ( )	**a.** to exclude
2. ban ( )	**b.** to get rid of; to abolish
3. sweeping ( )	**c.** to officially or legally prohibit
4. eliminate ( )	**d.** broad; wide-ranging
5. exempt ( )	**e.** limitation

B Fill in the blanks with appropriate expressions from the Vocabulary Check above. Change the word forms where necessary.

1. The new product does not completely (   ) bad odors, but it greatly reduces them.

2. As a result of the demonstrations, the government has proposed (   ) changes.

3. (   ) foreign workers from paying taxes allowed for the creation of a large work force.

4. Anyone who is caught drinking alcohol will be (   ) from the Youth Center.

5. Anyone can become a member! There are no (   ) at all.

News Story [1' 55"]

W. Johnson: We move on now to those new restrictions on vaping products. The FDA banning the sale of most kinds of flavored e-cigarette cartridges. But the plan   5
backs off of the more sweeping changes President Trump first proposed. And health officials say it doesn't go far enough 1. _____
_____. Here's ABC's Linsey Davis.

L. Davis: Tonight, the Food and Drug Administration announcing a partial ban   10
on some flavored e-cigarettes in an attempt to curb teenage and youth vaping. But critics say it does not go far enough.

M. Myers, President, Campaign for Tobacco-Free Kids: It would be wrong to say that this is 2. _____.

L. Davis: The proposal eliminates mint, fruit, and dessert-flavored e-cigarette   15
cartridges, but it still allows menthol and tobacco flavors, and does not address liquids sold in vape shops.

M. Myers: By exempting menthol e-cigarettes and 3. _____
_____, it's a loophole big enough to drive a truck through and it won't work.   20

L. Davis: According to recent studies, five million middle and high school students use e-cigarettes. In September, President Trump vowed to do something, quote, "very, very strong about it."

5

President D. Trump: It's, again, very new and potentially very bad. There have been deaths. And **4.** _____

_____.

L. Davis: But earlier this week, he sent more of a mixed message.

10

D. Trump: We have to protect the children. We have to protect the families. At the same time, we have a very big industry. It's become a very big industry. We're gonna take care of the industry.

L. Davis: The president of the American Lung Association **5.** _____

_____, saying, they are, quote, "sad to see an industry-supported approach take precedence over our kids' lung health."

15

W. Johnson: And Linsey Davis joining us here in studio. Linsey, this plan, the ban is just temporary, though.

L. Davis: Right. Yeah, this ban is FDA policy for now, but the administration's really leaving the door open for the products to be sold, **6.** _____

_____. But at this point,

20

manufacturers have 30 days to stop making the affected flavors, Whit.

W. Johnson: All right, Linsey, thank you.

Notes   **vaping products**「ベイパー製品〈vapor（蒸気）を発生させる製品。電子たばこ（e-cigarette）のこと。たばこ葉を用いず，一般的にニコチンを含む液体を加熱して，蒸気を発生させて吸入する〉」 **FDA**「食品医薬品局〈Food and Drug Administration〉」 **backs off of ~**「～から後退する；～を撤回する」 **health officials**「保健当局者」 **Campaign for Tobacco-Free Kids**「たばこの影響を受けない子どもたちのためのキャンペーン」 **dessert-flavored**「（キャンディーなど）デザート風味の」 **address**「対応する；言及する；対象とする；扱う」 **loophole**「（法や規制などの）抜け穴」 **vowed**「～を誓った；明言した；公約した」 **American Lung Association**「アメリカ肺協会」 **take precedence over ~**「～より優先する」 **affected flavors**「規制の対象になった風味のたばこ」

Background of the News

　トランプ米大統領は 2019 年 12 月, 電子たばこ (e-cigarette) を含むたばこ製品の購入可能年齢を, 現行の 18 歳から 21 歳に引き上げる法案に署名した。それ以前から, 喫煙年齢は, 多くの州で 21 歳とされていた。また, アメリカでは飲酒年齢も 1988 年までに全ての州で 21 歳になっている。

　電子たばこは「ベイパー製品」(vaping products) と呼ばれ, 専用カートリッジ内の液体を電気で熱して霧状にして吸う仕組みである。ニコチン入りが主流だがデザート風味 (dessert-flavored) の香料を含む溶液を加えるなど, 吸いやすさを売りに, 特に若者の人気を集めている。

　米疾病予防センター (CDC) の調査によると, アメリカで電子たばこを吸っている中高生は 2019 年に 500 万人超にのぼり, その多くがカートリッジ型のフレーバー製品を使っていた。蒸気自体は無臭なので, 学校などで隠れて吸っても見つかりにくいという。

　最近, アメリカでは電子たばこによる重篤な健康被害が相次いで報告されている。2019 年 10 月 31 日付の『日本経済新聞』(朝刊) によると, 2019 年 9 月以降, アメリカで電子たばこ製品使用による急性肺疾患の報告が急増し, これまでに 2,500 人が入院, 50 人が死亡し, 患者の約 4 割は 20 歳以下の若者だという。

　今回, 若者の使用は少ないとされるメンソールやたばこ風味 (menthol and tobacco flavors) は規制の対象から外れた。トランプ大統領が電子たばこの全面禁止に踏み込まなかったのは, 2020 年 11 月の大統領選への影響を考慮したからと見られている。

After　You Watch the News

Exercises

A Listen to the CD and fill in the blanks in the text.　　　◎ CD 05

B Multiple Choice Questions

1. The proposed ban on vaping products
   a. is not permanent.
   b. affects some but not all flavors.
   c. both *a* and *b*

2. The FDA's ban

    a. applies only to middle and high school students.

    b. has been criticized by the American Lung Association.

    c. is based on President Trump's initial reform proposal.

3. Compared to his position in September, President Trump is now

    a. more supportive of the tobacco industry.

    b. more intent on closing all of the loopholes.

    c. more in agreement with the Campaign for Tobacco-Free Kids.

4. Which of the following is **NOT** true of e-cigarettes?

    a. They are used by millions of American teenagers.

    b. A variety of new flavors are currently being manufactured.

    c. Types exempt from the ban will stop being made in 30 days.

C **Translate the following Japanese into English. Then listen to the CD and practice the conversation with your partner.** CD 06

A: 1. _____.

B: Not all of them. You can still get the tobacco and menthol flavors.

A: But I like the flavored cartridges. Mint is my favorite.

B: 2. Hey,_____. What happened?

A: I did for a month or so, but I missed it. It's a nice way to relax.

B: 3. Well,_____. Vaping has caused deaths, you know.

A: Oh, come on. You sound like my mother. Everybody's doing it!

1. 電子たばこを禁止するなんて信じられません。

2. ねえ，先学期にベイピングをやめたと思っていました。

3. まあ，またやめるにはいい時期かもしれませんね。

D Summary Practice: Fill in the blanks with suitable words beginning with the letters indicated.

⊙ CD 07

A new (¹· **b**   ) is about to be implemented in the U.S. that will place
(²· **r**   ) on the sale of e-cigarettes. Although President
Trump once expressed his belief in the need for (³· **s**   )
changes to curb the habit that has resulted in (⁴· **d**   ), he has now
backed down. The sale of (⁵· **f**   ) (⁶· **c**   )
will no longer be allowed, but the legislation has some strong critics because
it (⁷· **e**   ) menthol e-cigarettes and (⁸· **l**   ) sold in
(⁹· **v**   ) (¹⁰· **s**   ). Among them is the (¹¹· **C**   )
for Tobacco-Free Kids, who protest that the ban will not go far enough to
(¹²· **c**   ) the youth (¹³· **v**   ) problem. With an estimated
(¹⁴· **f**   ) (¹⁵· **m**   ) middle and high school students said to be
using e-cigarettes, the American Lung Association is also critical of the
president for siding with an (¹⁶· **i**   )-(¹⁷· **s**   )
approach with too many (¹⁸· **l**   ) over the health of
America's youth.

E Discussion: Share your ideas and opinions with your classmates.

1. How much do you know about e-cigarettes and vaping? Do an Internet
search and see what you can learn.

2. What do you think about bans on products like these? Does the
government have the right to decide what people can and can't do?
Should people be allowed to make their own decisions?

3. Look for statistics on e-cigarette consumption in Japan. How common is
it? Is vaping becoming more or less popular? Are there any regulations on
sales?

　gonna と wanna は，それぞれ going to, want to の略式表現，縮約形として知られている。標準的な口語表現なので，くだけた会話に限定して使用されると思われがちであるが，gonna の方は，以下の例のようにニュースのアンカーパーソン，また公式な場でアメリカ大統領や米軍司令官なども使う。

— **D. Trump:** It's become a very big industry. We're ***gonna*** take care of the industry.　　　　　　　　　　　　*(E-Cigarette: Partial Ban Backlash, p.8)*

— **T. Llamas:** So Jim decided, at least in his community of Sanford, North Carolina, that wasn't ***gonna*** happen.

(The Veteran and His Homemade Toys, p.14)

— **J. Miller, Deputy Commissioner, Intelligence & Counterterrorism:** Times Square is probably ***gonna*** be…　　*(Security from Above, p.31)*

— **U.S. military commander:** If neither side's ***gonna*** win it militarily, you have to move into a, towards a political settlement here.

(Ending the War?, p.50)

— **D. Muir:** *We're **gonna** stay on this.*

(Volunteers Feeding Those in Need, p.85)

The Veteran and His Homemade Toys

You Watch the News

Air Date: December 23, 2019
Duration: 1' 57"

Preview Questions

1. Who is Jim Annis?
 ——ジム・アニスさんはどのような人ですか。
2. Why does he make toys?
 ——なぜ，彼はおもちゃを作っているのですか。

Warm-up Exercises

A **Vocabulary Check: Choose the correct definition for each of the words below.**

1. veteran (   )
2. scrap (   )
3. makeshift (   )
4. assemble (   )
5. air (   )

a. to put together
b. temporary; sufficient for the time being
c. a person who has had experience in the war
d. to broadcast on television or the radio
e. a small left-over piece

B Fill in the blanks with appropriate expressions from the Vocabulary Check above. Change the word forms where necessary.

1. Our dog always comes looking for food (   ) when we are eating dinner.
2. We really like the new desk, but it was hard to (   ).
3. The whole school was excited when our music teacher's original song was (   ) for the first time.
4. My grandfather was a (   ) of two wars.
5. What was intended as a (   ) office served us well for almost three years.

News Story [1' 57"]

T. Llamas: Finally tonight, the veteran and his homemade toys, showing us all the real meaning of Christmas. It's "America Strong."

Day in and day out, just like Santa, 80-year-old Jim Annis is working under deadline, getting all these handmade toys out by Christmas day. This is Jim's second act in life. The first, [1.] _____ _____ in the Korean War. But it was even before that, Jim's life mission started taking shape.

J. Annis: My dad, he worked, but he didn't make a whole lot of money and with five kids, it's so hard to have a very big Christmas.

T. Llamas: [2.] _____ but not getting any during the holidays is something Jim says you never forget. So Jim decided, at least in his community of Sanford, North Carolina, that wasn't gonna happen.

J. Annis: When the Salvation Army gives out the food and the clothes to the people in this area, I give out my toys.

T. Llamas: Collecting scraps of wood [3.] _____, sweating hours in his makeshift toy factory, assembling 300 toys,

5

10

15

20

distributed through the Salvation
Army. Jim covers the cost of the
machinery, paint and accessories.
Jim's story first aired on our
Raleigh station, WTVD. Since
then, *4.* _____

_____.

J. Annis: You have people from California to Texas, ah... way off there, I've
never dreamed would even hear about my story.

T. Llamas: And oh, what a story. The little boy *5.* _____

_____, now giving

so much and getting more gifts than he could ever imagine.

J. Annis: People ask me, how much do I get paid for making these toys? And
ah... I say, my pay is when I see the smile on the kids' faces.

T. Llamas: Jim, you're making us all smile. Thank you so much for watching.
I'm Tom Llamas in New York. See you on *GMA* first thing tomorrow
morning and right back here tomorrow night. Have a great evening.
Good night.

Notes **America Strong** 「アメリカ・ストロング〈*ABC World News Tonight* には America Strong（強く
あれ，アメリカ）という心温まるニュース，アメリカを元気にしてくれるニュースを紹介するコーナー
がある〉」　**Day in and day out** 「毎日毎日；来る日も来る日も；明けても暮れても」　**getting ～ out** 「～
を（完成して）出荷する；～を届ける」　**second act** 「（人生の）第二幕〈人の役に立つような行動を
起こすのが 2 回目〉」　**the Korean War** 「朝鮮戦争〈1950 年に北朝鮮と韓国との間で生じた朝鮮半島
の主権を巡る戦争。1953 年に休戦協定が締結されて以来，北緯 38 度線を境に大韓民国と朝鮮民主主
義人民共和国の南北二国に分断された〉」　**Sanford** 「サンフォード〈ノースカロライナ州中部の都市〉」
Salvation Army 「サルベーション・アーミー；救世軍〈資金を集めるために寄贈品や中古品の衣類，
家具，書籍などを安く販売しているキリスト教の団体〉」　**sweating hours** 「何時間も汗を流して（作
業して）」　**Raleigh station, WTVD** 「WTVD のローリーテレビ〈WTVD は，ノースカロライナ州の州
都ローリーなどを受信エリアとする ABC 系列のローカルテレビ局〉」　**way off there** 「ずっと遠い所か
ら」　**I've never dreamed would even hear about my story.** 「（そんな遠い場所に住んでいる人が）
私の話を聞いてくれるとは夢にも思っていなかった。〈文法的に逸脱している。次のように言いたかっ
たと思われる。I never dreamed that people so far away as Texas and California would hear my
story.〉」　**GMA** 「グッドモーニング・アメリカ（*Good Morning America*）〈アメリカ ABC 放送のモ
ーニングショー〉」

Exercises

A Listen to the CD and fill in the blanks in the text.

CD 08

B Multiple Choice Questions

1. When he was a child, Jim Annis
   a. didn't receive any toys for Christmas.
   b. received homemade toys for Christmas.
   c. received more gifts than he could imagine.

2. Which of the following is *TRUE* about Jim Annis?
   a. When he was young, his father was unemployed.
   b. Fighting in the war inspired him to begin making toys.
   c. Due to his own childhood situation, he now gives away toys.

3. The toys that Jim makes
   a. are sold only to local families.
   b. will soon start being sold all around the U.S.
   c. are given to needy children in his community.

4. What kind of support does Jim get for his project?
   a. a salary from the Salvation Army
   b. free paint and accessories from construction sites
   c. donations from people who hear about his story

C Translate the following Japanese into English. Then listen to the CD and practice the conversation with your partner. ◉ CD 09

A: Hey, Jim! We're going bowling tomorrow. Can you join us?

B: I'm afraid not. ¹· _____ , you know.

A: But Christmas is still a month away. And it's the weekend!

B: I still have 50 wooden toys to assemble. I can't disappoint the kids.

A: ²· _____
_____ , by the way?

B: I get paid in smiles! Making children happy on Christmas is worth more than money.

A: ³· _____ .
Maybe I'll skip bowling and help you out.

1. 締め切りが迫っていますからね。

2. ところで，その手作りおもちゃでいくら貰えるのですか。

3. たぶん，それがクリスマスの本当の意味なのですね。

D Summary Practice: Fill in the blanks with suitable words beginning with the letters indicated. ◉ CD 10

Although he doesn't have a white beard or wear a red suit, (¹· e   )-year-old Jim Annis is (²· S   ) to many children in his (³· c   ) of Sanford, (⁴· N   ) (⁵· C   ). Growing up in a large family with (⁶· f   ) children, Jim's parents couldn't afford a big (⁷· C   ). After fighting in the (⁸· K   ) (⁹· W   ), Jim took on a new (¹⁰· m   ): making (¹¹· w   ) toys for children whose parents can't buy them presents. Using (¹²· s   ) of wood from (¹³· c   ) sites, Jim works (¹⁴· d   ) (¹⁵· i   ) and day out in his (¹⁶· m   ) factory to make hundreds of toys,which are distributed by the (¹⁷· S   ) (¹⁸· A   ). Although Jim has always paid for the (¹⁹· m   ), paint and (²⁰· a   ) himself, after his story (²¹· a   ) on television, he has been receiving (²²· d   ) from all across the U.S. His childhood Christmases may have been (²³· s   ), but for Jim Annis, the (²⁴· s   ) on the faces of the kids who receive his toys are the best (²⁵· g   ) ever.

E **Discussion: Share your ideas and opinions with your classmates.**

1. Look for other stories about people who found creative ways to improve the quality of life in their communities. Have you or someone you know ever taken part in such activities? Would you like to?

2. Receiving toys from Santa is a precious childhood memory for many people. Share stories about your Christmas memories. What was the best Christmas present you ever got?

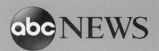

To the Moon

Air Date: February 24, 2020
Duration: 2' 02"

Preview Questions

1. Who was Katherine Johnson?
——キャサリン・ジョンソンとはどのような人物でしたか。

2. Why was she considered to be a pioneer?
——なぜ彼女は先駆者とみなされていたのですか。

Warm-up Exercises

A Vocabulary Check: Choose the correct definition for each of the words below.

1. man （ ）

2. calculate （ ）

3. precise （ ）

4. gal （ ）

5. civilian （ ）

a. exact

b. a person who is not in the military

c. slang for girl or woman

d. to compute; to work out

e. to operate; to drive

B Fill in the blanks with appropriate expressions from the Vocabulary Check above. Change the word forms where necessary.

1. Let's have the guys sit here and the (   ), over there.
2. Kim was happy to get the job, but rather disappointed when she (   ) what her annual salary would be.
3. Your explanation is too vague. You should try to be more (   ).
4. Who will (   ) the plane if all of the pilots are on strike?
5. Under normal circumstances, no (   ) are allowed to enter the building.

News Story [2′ 02″]

D. Muir: Finally tonight here, "America Strong." An American pioneer who, for so long, was a hidden figure at NASA.

Katherine Johnson was from West Virginia. She was a mathematician, a pioneer. Part of a small group of African-American women hired as mathematicians at NASA. Breaking gender barriers, racial barriers in the '50s and '60s, she worked on the first U.S. manned space flights.

NASA controller: We have a liftoff.

D. Muir: Calculating the precise trajectories that would allow Apollo 11 ¹·_____ _____.

N. Armstrong, astronaut: That's one small step for man, one giant leap for mankind.

D. Muir: Her role was long overlooked. Katherine on the far right. Her daughter would hear the stories.

Daughter: Momma got there at '53. The engineers came and ²· _____ _____. The supervisor said, "Oh, well, that's Katherine."

D. Muir: And what was her role?

Daughter: The work was to take a
    Monroe or a Friden calculator and
    do the big equations, which could
    be a page long.

T. P. Henson, actress: [3] _____

_____.

D. Muir: Johnson's role portrayed in the film *Hidden Figures*.

K. Dunst, actress: You have someone?

O. Spencer, actress: Oh, yes, ma'am. Katherine's the gal for that. She can
    handle any numbers you put in front of her.

D. Muir: She would own her role.

T. P. Henson: We can calculate launch and landing. But without this
    conversion, the capsule stays in orbit. [4] _____
    _____.

D. Muir: You'll remember the movie was nominated for best picture.

T. P. Henson: A true NASA and American hero, Katherine Johnson.

D. Muir: She was also awarded the Presidential Medal of Freedom, the nation's
    highest civilian honor. And when her daughter asked all those years
    later, what if someone questioned you?

Daughter: What happened if somebody questioned your work?

K. Johnson, mathematician: Tough.

D. Muir: Tough. And so was she. [5] _____
    _____.

    Katherine Johnson was 101 and an American original. I'm David Muir.
    Good night.

Notes **NASA**「ナサ；アメリカ航空宇宙局〈＝ National Aeronautics and Space Administration〉」 **trajectories**「軌道」 **at '53**「1953 年に〈文法的には *in* '53〉」 **supervisor**「主任」 **a Monroe or a Friden calculator**「モンローやフリーデンの（計算機）〈両者ともアメリカの電動計算機のメーカーで，1960 年代に電子式計算機（電卓）が普及する前の計算機〉」 **equations**「方程式」 ***Hidden Figures***「ドリーム（邦題）〈2016 年にアメリカ合衆国で公開された映画〉」 **conversion**「変換式〈=conversion equation〉」 **Presidential Medal of Freedom**「大統領自由勲章〈アメリカ文民最高位にあたる勲章で，世界平和，文化活動などに貢献した人物を対象に，大統領が授与する〉」

After You Watch the News

Exercises

A Listen to the CD and fill in the blanks in the text. CD 11

B Multiple Choice Questions

1. Katherine Johnson
   a. was known as the first African American astronaut.
   b. was respected for the work she did in mathematics.
   c. was famous for appearing in an award-nominated film.

2. Which of the following is ***NOT*** true about Katherine Johnson?
   a. She was the recipient of America's highest civilian award.
   b. The important work she did was not recognized for a long time.
   c. She was the only African American woman working for NASA.

3. In the 1950s and 1960s, NASA
   a. was not yet considering manned flights.
   b. did not feel that mathematics was important.
   c. broke racial and gender barriers in their hiring.

4. Which statement below best describes Johnson's work?
   a. She performed complicated calculations that made it possible for astronauts to go to space.
   b. She discovered the equations that were needed to build the Apollo 11 spacecraft.
   c. She successfully calculated the trajectory of the first NASA spacecraft to go into space.

C Translate the following Japanese into English. Then listen to the CD and practice the conversation with your partner.   ◎ CD12

A: Hidden Figures is showing at the mall. Shall we go see it?

B: I've never heard of it. What's it about?

A: 1. It's an amazing story about _____

_____ .

B: Way back then? What did they do?

A: They were mathematicians. 2. _____

_____ .

B: That's amazing! How come I've never heard of her?

A: 3. _____

_____ . Shall we go see the film?

B: Let's go right now!

1. 1950 年代に NASA に雇われた少人数のアフリカ系アメリカ人女性たちの驚くべき物語ですよ。

2. そのうちの一人，キャサリン・ジョンソンは，宇宙飛行の軌道解析をしました。

3. 彼女の重要な業績は，実は長い間見落とされていたのです。

D Summary Practice: Fill in the blanks with suitable words beginning with the letters indicated.   ◎ CD 13

Katherine Johnson, a (1. **m**   ) with NASA, has died at the ripe old age of 101. A recipient of the (2. **P**   ) (3. **M**   ) of (4. **F**   ), Johnson broke both (5. **g**   ) and (6. **r**   ) barriers when working for the organization in the 1950s and '60s. A native of (7. **W**   ) (8. **V**   ), Johnson was part of a small group of math specialists hired specifically to aid the (9. **e**   ) by doing complicated (10. **e**   ). Johnson's amazing work enabled them to calculate how to bring a space (11. **c**   ) back to earth, resulting in the first (12. **m**   ) space flights. The story of Katherine Johnson and the mathematicians who worked with her are the subject of the highly acclaimed film (13. **H**   ) (14. **F**   ).

E **Discussion: Share your ideas and opinions with your classmates.**

1. How much do you know about NASA? Do an Internet search to find out about the organization's history and current projects.

2. Do you know of other African American trailblazers? Choose one of the people listed below and find out why they were felt to be pioneers for the African American community.

     Jo Ann Robinson   Madam C.J. Walker   Bessie Coleman

3. If you can, watch the film *Hidden Figures*. Look for specific examples of the discrimination faced by Katherine Johnson and her African American colleagues.

Flooding in Venice

Before You Watch the News

Air Date: November 24, 2019
Duration: 1' 23"

Preview Questions

1. What is the situation in Venice?
   ——ベネチアはどのような状態ですか。

2. What are some of the effects of the flooding?
   ——浸水はどのような影響をもたらしていますか。

Warm-up Exercises

A Vocabulary Check: Choose the correct definition for each of the words below.

1. devastated ( )
2. wade ( )
3. submerged ( )
4. unprecedented ( )
5. donation ( )

a. never seen before
b. money or other items given for a cause
c. to walk through water
d. state of being under water
e. destroyed; ruined

B Fill in the blanks with appropriate expressions from the Vocabulary Check above. Change the word forms where necessary.

1. An (   ) number of visitors are expected for the annual exhibition.
2. The Boy Scouts are collecting (   ) throughout the state to build a school in Manila.
3. Timmy can't swim yet, but he loves (   ) in the kiddie pool.
4. A number of homes were (   ) by the recent earthquake.
5. We were shocked to find that many cars were completely (   ) in water following the heavy rains.

News Story [1' 23"]

T. Llamas: To the new round of devastating flooding in Venice. People in one of the world's most famous cities, wading through waters from their ankles all the way to their knees. Protests now breaking out as ^{1.} _____

_____. ABC's Maggie Rulli is in Venice.

M. Rulli: Tonight, Venice and some of its most famous landmarks submerged again as the city struggles with weeks of unprecedented and deadly flooding.

^{2.} _____ and they're expecting St. Mark's Square to stay flooded like this for the rest of the week.

Water inundating this iconic landmark, damaging homes and businesses nearby. The mayor saying it could cost more than a billion dollars to repair. Reports of as many as a third of visitors cancelling their trips. Locals agree ^{3.}_____.

Protester: (Speaking in Italian)

M. Rulli: Hundreds taking to the streets. Many say they are fearful for their city's future.

Resident: Venice is literally drowning and the water is rising.

M. Rulli: During the worst of the flooding, this man was swimming. Suitcases floating like gondolas. **4.**_____ 5

_____ as Venice tries to keep its businesses running.

Tonight, we're dealing with another high tide and more flooding here in 10 St. Mark's Square. And we're expecting to see a repeat of this scene again and again over the next few days. Tom, **5.**_____ _____ that the local government has even started asking for international donations to help. Tom?

Notes   **new round**「新しい展開（局面）」   **St. Mark's Square**「サンマルコ広場」   **iconic landmark**「象徴的なランドマーク（観光名所；史跡）」   **taking to the streets**「街頭に出て抗議のデモをする」   **local government**「地元政府（自治体）」

Background of the News

　「水の都」として知られる世界遺産のベネチアが水没の危機にさらされている。ニュース映像に出てくるように，高潮が押し寄せたサンマルコ広場 (St. Mark's Square) で，観光客が渡し板を歩く姿は，毎年のように繰り返される光景になってきた。住宅に浸水被害が出る高潮(high tide)は，1980 年代に年平均 2.6 回起きていたのが，最近の 10 年間は年平均 8.2 回に大幅に増えている。

　2019 年 11 月 15 付の『日本経済新聞』によると，イタリア政府は 14 日に，大規模な浸水被害が発生したことを受け，非常事態宣言を発令した。最高水位は 187 センチに達し，市内の 8 割以上が浸水したという。ベネチア地元当局 (local government) は今回，1966 年に次ぐ観測史上 2 番目に高い水位となったと発表した。今回の高潮では，観光客が集まるサンマルコ広場や象徴的な観光名所 (iconic landmark) が広範囲にわたって浸水した。気候変動 (climate change) が原因とされている。

　ベネチアでは，高潮を防ぐために水門の設置など，約 55 億ユーロ（約 6,600 億円）をかけ，大規模な国家プロジェクトとして防潮対策事業が 2003 年に始まった。このプロジェクトは現在も進行中で，汚職や建設費の高騰などで大幅な遅延を余儀なくされたものの，2020 年 7 月には水門の作動テストが行われた。

After | You Watch the News

Exercises

A Listen to the CD and fill in the blanks in the text.　　　　　◎ CD 14

B Mark the following sentences true (T) or false (F) according to the information in the news story.

(　) **1.** The flooding in Venice has been going on for weeks.

(　) **2.** Only the most iconic landmarks are being protected from the floods.

(　) **3.** The mayor of Venice estimates that it could cost over a billion dollars to repair the damage.

(　) **4.** Half of the people who had been planning to visit Venice have cancelled their trips.

(　) **5.** Some people believe that the floods are the result of climate change.

(　) **6.** The Italian government has asked foreign countries for financial aid.

C Translate the following Japanese into English. Then listen to the CD and practice the conversation with your partner.　　　　◎ CD 15

A: What are we going to do? They're expecting more flooding in St. Mark's Square.

B: I think the smartest thing is to cancel our trip.

A: ¹· But _____!

B: You don't want to go all the way to Italy to see Venice submerged under water, do you?

A: I guess you've got a point.

B: ²· And _____

_____.

A: The devastation is awful. Okay—³· _____

_____.

1. でも，ベネチアの象徴的なランドマークを見るのは，ずっと夢だったのですよ。

2. それに，膝まで水につかりながらデモをしている人たちのことを考えてみてくださいよ。

3. 旅行をキャンセルして寄付金を送ろう。

28

D Summary Practice: Fill in the blanks with suitable words beginning with
the letters indicated.   ◎ CD 16

The world-famous city of (¹· **V**   ) is currently suffering from the
effects of (²· **u**   ) (³· **f**   ).
With (⁴· **i**   ) landmarks (⁵· **s**   ) and water
(⁶· **i**   ) St. Mark's (⁷· **S**   ), (⁸· **p**   )
are now breaking out among the (⁹· **l**   ). Amid scenes of people
(¹⁰· **s**   ) in the streets and suitcases floating like
(¹¹· **g**   ), many are fearful for the (¹²· **f**   ) of their
city. With (¹³· **r**   ) estimated at a (¹⁴· **b**   ) dollars and a
(¹⁵· **t**   ) of all visitors (¹⁶· **c**   ) their trips, the
(¹⁷· **l**   ) government has begun to ask for international
(¹⁸· **d**   ). Venice is yet another victim of (¹⁹· **c**   )
(²⁰· **c**   ).

E Discussion: Share your ideas and opinions with your classmates.

1. According to the news story, many people blame the unprecedented
   flooding on climate change. Discuss with your classmates other examples
   of devastating weather conditions attributed to climate change. Can you
   think of any cases in Japan?
2. Find out more about what you can see and do in the city of Venice. If you
   were to plan a trip there from Japan, how could you get there? Check out
   which airlines offer flights to that region of Italy, and how much it would
   cost.

News Story 6

Security from Above

Air Date: December 31, 2019
Duration: 1' 32"

Preview Questions

1. Why are drones being used in New York City?
——なぜニューヨークでドローンが使われているのですか。

2. In addition to drones, what other measures are being taken to protect the crowds?
——ドローンの他，群衆を守るためにどのような対策がとられていますか。

Warm-up Exercises

A Vocabulary Check: Choose the correct definition for each of the words below.

1. sniff (　　)

2. credible (　　)

3. ensure (　　)

4. unauthorized (　　)

5. massive (　　)

a. believable; quite certain

b. extremely large

c. to make certain

d. not having official permission or approval

e. to breathe in to detect a smell

B **Fill in the blanks with appropriate expressions from the Vocabulary Check above. Change the word forms where necessary.**

1. A (   ) rock was blocking the path, so we had to leave our car and walk.

2. Saying that your dog was sick is not a (   ) excuse for not doing your assignment.

3. Why is the dog (   ) at your feet?

4. The school is distributing hand sanitizer in order to help (   ) good hygiene.

5. (   ) use of the new computers is strictly forbidden.

News Story [1' 32"]

W. Johnson: One million people are expected to pack into Times Square for the iconic ball drop there. Crowds streaming in at this hour. The NYPD out in full force, launching new high-tech equipment overhead. Here's ABC's Adrienne Bankert.

5

A. Bankert: Tonight, ^{1.} _____ on New Year's Eve, specialized drones will be dotting the skies over New York to   10 protect one of the world's biggest celebrations.

J. Miller, Deputy Commissioner, Intelligence & Counterterrorism: Times Square is probably gonna be ^{2.} _____ _____.

A. Bankert: About a million people will pack Times Square. First going through   15 several layers of security, including metal detectors and bomb-sniffing dogs. Authorities say there is no specific credible threat, but thousands of NYPD officers ^{3.} _____ _____.

T. Monahan, Chief, NYPD: You have all these resources on the ground. Our   20 aviation unit will be overhead, surveying rooftops and ensuring the crowds are safe.

A. Bankert: 4. _____

_____,

there are police monitoring more
than 1,200 cameras, as well as
feeds from helicopters and those
drones. The NYPD also has the capability to block unauthorized drones
from above Times Square. And on the ground, blockades of huge trucks
creating a ring of steel.

J. Miller: Nobody else puts that kind of effort into an event like this.

A. Bankert: And here's one more note about those drones. These, again, are
highly specialized. They are equipped with thermal imaging, 3-D
mapping technology and the ability to zoom in on anything on the
ground. You can see a lot going on right behind us. One of those massive
trucks we talked about and a huge line of people 5. _____

_____. We hope everyone

is safe.

5

10

15

Notes   **ball drop**「ボールドロップ〈タイムズスクエアのビル，ワン・タイムズスクエアの屋上には巨大なク
リスタルボールが設置されている。ポールにくし刺しされたようになっているそのボールは，徐々にポー
ルを降り始め，0時ピッタリに42メートルほど降下し，新年の始まりを告げる。その瞬間，周囲の
高層ビルから紙吹雪が舞い，そのイベントがニューヨークの大晦日のシンボルになっている〉」 **NYPD**
「ニューヨーク市警〈New York City Police Department〉」 **dotting**「（空中に）点在する」 **Deputy
Commissioner, Intelligence & Counterterrorism**「情報・テロ対策担当副長官」 **bomb-sniffing
dogs**「爆弾探知犬；爆発物探知犬」 **resources**「（警備のための）資源；要員」 **aviation unit**「（警
備用ヘリコプターなどの）航空隊」 **feeds**「映像（情報）」 **ring of steel**「鉄壁の封鎖」 **thermal
imaging, 3-D mapping technology**「赤外線画像，3Dマッピング（撮影）技術」

After   You Watch the News

Exercises

A Listen to the CD and fill in the blanks in the text.   ⊙ CD 17

B Multiple Choice Questions

1. On New Year's Eve, Times Square will
   a. host an iconic ball game.
   b. probably be the safest place on Earth.
   c. draw huge crowds to see its high tech equipment.

2. Which of the following is **NOT** a protective measure planned for the event?
   a. an aviation unit watching from above
   b. metal detectors and bomb-sniffing dogs
   c. a million NYPD officers with heavy weapons

3. According to the NYPD
   a. this level of security is now normal in the U.S.
   b. only New York City has a high level of security all the time.
   c. this use of drones and other special measures is highly unusual.

4. Visitors to Times Square are expecting
   a. specific credible threats.
   b. resources on the ground and in the sky.
   c. unauthorized drones overhead.

C Translate the following Japanese into English. Then listen to the CD and practice the conversation with your partner. ⊙ CD 18

A: Care to join us tonight? We're heading to Times Square.
B: 1. _____, but not this year. It's too risky.
A: Are you kidding? New York has never been safer!
B: What do you mean?
A: Well, 2. _____
_____.
C: 3. _____
_____.
B: The NYPD has really gone all out! Okay, I'll join you. It sounds safer than staying home.

1. 真夜中に，象徴的なボールドロップを見るのが大好きです。
2. 今年は，1,200 台以上のカメラを備えた特別指令センターを設置しています。
3. 地上のものは何でもズームインできるハイテクドローンもあります。

D Summary Practice: Fill in the blanks with suitable words beginning with the letters indicated.

A big part of the preparation for the annual New Year's Eve event in
(¹· **T**   ) (²· **S**   ) involves (³· **e**   ) the safety
of those participating in one of the world's biggest (⁴· **c**   ).
With one million revelers expected to be in New York City for the
(⁵· **i**   ) ball drop at midnight, the authorities have for the first time
prepared specialized (⁶· **h**   )-(⁷· **t**   ) equipment to watch from
overhead. Visitors can expect several layers of (⁸· **s**   ) and
thousands of NYPD officers with (⁹· **w**   ) on the ground, but
specialized (¹⁰· **d**   ) with thermal (¹¹· **i**   ) will also
be keeping them (¹²· **s**   ) from the (¹³· **s**   ) above. The
Deputy Commissioner of Intelligence and Counterterrorism notes that even
though there is no specific (¹⁴· **c**   ) threat, it's no surprise that
New York is putting such great effort into the event.

E Discussion: Share your ideas and opinions with your classmates.

1. Drones have many uses, some of them controversial. See what you can find out about how they work and what they are used for. Why have they been in the news in recent years?
2. Watching the ball drop in Times Square is one important part of New Year's Eve for many Americans. How do you spend New Year's Eve? Do Japanese families have any special traditions?
3. The New Year's Eve ball drop in Times Square is an iconic symbol of New York City. What are some iconic images of Tokyo? Of your hometown?

No Limits Café

Air Date: February 21, 2020
Duration: 2' 07"

Preview Questions

1. What is special about the No Limits Café?
　——ノーリミッツ・カフェの特徴は何ですか。

2. How have people reacted to it?
　——それに対する人々の反応はどうですか。

Warm-up Exercises

A Vocabulary Check: Choose the correct definition for each of the words below.

1. device ( )　　　　**a.** tendency; movement
2. potential ( )　　　**b.** piece of equipment
3. all in ( )　　　　**c.** possibilities; promise
4. trend ( )　　　　**d.** providing equal access to opportunities
5. inclusive ( )　　　**e.** with great determination

B Fill in the blanks with appropriate expressions from the Vocabulary Check above. Change the word forms where necessary.

1. The detective planted a listening (   ) in the suspect's hotel room.
2. The students were (   ) when it came to preparing a surprise retirement party for their teacher.
3. His music teacher feels that Tom has great (   ) to become a professional pianist.
4. Her sister always keeps up with the latest fashion (   ), but Pam doesn't have much interest in clothes.
5. Club membership there is not as (   ) as it seems. They don't accept anyone without a college degree.

News Story [2′ 07″]

D. Muir: Finally, tonight here, our "Persons of the Week." The workers and their bosses determined to make sure they get a chance.

In Middletown, New Jersey, the No Limits Café means just what it says.

5

S. Cartier, owner, No Limits Café: Hi, David. Welcome to No Limits Café in Middletown, New Jersey. ¹· _____.

D. Muir: Stephanie Cartier employs dozens of workers with special needs.

10

Employee 1: I'm gonna be your server.

D. Muir: Amanda bringing out the drinks. Tommy in the kitchen. Jake, taking orders.

Employee 1: May I get you guys anything to drink?

D. Muir: And ²· _____, their boss saying there are no limits.

15

S. Cartier: You can be non-verbal, you use a mobile device, like a wheelchair or a walker, we don't care 'cause everybody has potential. Everybody.

5

D. Muir: Stephanie's daughter Katie has special needs.

S. Cartier: We have a daughter who has Down syndrome. What is she gonna do after high school when she turns 21?

D. Muir: She thought, 3. _____ and so many other sons and daughters, too.

10

Employee 2: I love this job. And hopefully, like, it's keep getting more and more people come in.

Employee 3: Everyone's here is so positive and, like, gets you in the mood to work.

15

D. Muir: And the customers are all in.

Customer 1: I think it's a really great idea.

Customer 2: I hope it's a trend, because there is a large community of special needs adults.

D. Muir: We hope so, too. In fact, 4. _____ _____. There was Coleman in Dallas, Texas.

20

C. Jones, vice president, Howdy Homemade Ice Cream: Hi, David Muir, come on in.

D. Muir: He is vice president of Howdy Homemade Ice Cream.

Customer 3: What's this one?

25

Employee 4: Coffee and cookies.

Customer 3: Coffee and cookies, huh?

D. Muir: A dozen employees from 16 to 31, 5. _____

_____, too. And until this ice cream shop, Annemarie Kerrigan had trouble finding a job.

A. Kerrigan: It makes me feel like there's not a place in me in this world.

D. Muir: There is now, because Dallas businessman Tom Landis knew exactly the kind of workers he was looking for.

T. Landis, Howdy Homemade Ice Cream: It just jumped out that, hey,

6. _____

_____.

D. Muir: So, from Dallas to Middletown, New Jersey, tonight, it's the workers and their inclusive bosses setting the bar for the rest of us.

Employee 5: This one's for you, David Muir.

D. Muir: Looks good. And so, we choose tonight, every one of those workers and their bosses. Good night.

Notes **Person of the Week**「今週の人（のコーナー）〈番組では毎週，地域で貢献している人を「今週の人」として紹介している〉」 **Middletown**「ミドルタウン〈ニュージャージー州東部の郡区 (township)〉」 **special needs**「スペシャルニーズ；特別なニーズ；支援を必要とする障がい」 **no limits**「制限がない；限界がない」 **non-verbal**「言葉が使えない」 **walker**「ウォーカー〈歩行が困難な人のための歩行器具〉」 **And hopefully, like, it's keep getting more and more people come in.**「= And hopefully, like, *we'll* keep getting more and more people *coming* in.」 **Everyone's here is so positive**「= *Everyone here's* so positive」 **like**「その〜；まあ；何か〈つなぎ言葉として，くだけた会話の中でよく使われる〉」 **Dallas**「ダラス〈テキサス州北東部の都市〉」 **there's not a place in me**「自分の居場所がない〈there's not a place *for* me と言いたかったと思われる〉」 **It just jumped out that ~**「〜だと思った；〜に気がついた」 **setting the bar**「（障がい者雇用の）基準を設定する」

Exercises

A Listen to the CD and fill in the blanks in the text.   ◎ CD 20

B Mark the following sentences true (T) or false (F) according to the information in the news story.

(   ) **1.** The owner of the No Limits Café believes that everyone has potential.

(   ) **2.** The owner opened the café to help her daughter, who is non-verbal.

(   ) **3.** The employees are enjoying their jobs.

(   ) **4.** The vice president of Howdy Homemade Ice Cream was formerly a special needs teacher.

(   ) **5.** According to the news story, it is generally easy for young people with special needs to find work.

(   ) **6.** Both Stephanie Cartier and Tom Landis can be described as inclusive bosses.

C Translate the following Japanese into English. Then listen to the CD and practice the conversation with your partner.   ⊙ CD 21

A: What shall we do for lunch? How about McDonalds?

B: I have a better idea. Let's check out the No Limits Café.

A: Never heard of it. Isn't that a strange name for a restaurant?

B: It's not strange at all! ¹·_____

_____.

A: No kidding! Gee— ²· I wonder if _____

_____. He can't seem to find any work.

B: The owner is a really amazing woman. ³· _____

_____. He should check it out.

A: Okay, let's go there for lunch and afterwards, I'll talk to her about Toby.

1. 従業員全員が特別なニーズを持っています。

2. 私の近所の車いすを使っているあの男性を雇ってくれるかな。

3. 彼女は，すべての人に可能性があると信じています。

Summary Practice: Fill in the blanks with suitable words beginning with
   the letters indicated.   CD 22

ABC News has some outstanding candidates for their "(¹· **P**   )
of the Week": the (²· **w**   ) and (³· **b**   ) at the No Limits
(⁴· **C**   ) in New Jersey and Howdy (⁵· **H**   ) Ice Cream
in Dallas. What do these two shops have in common? Both employ people
with (⁶· **s**   ) (⁷· **n**   ) to work in the (⁸· **k**   ) and
serve (⁹· **c**   ). The owner of the café, Stephanie Cartier,
and (¹⁰· **T**   ) Landis of the ice cream shop are both (¹¹· **i**   )
in their hiring practices. According to Cartier, whose daughter has Down
(¹²· **s**   ), everybody has (¹³· **p**   ). Landis
knew the kind of workers the (¹⁴· **r**   ) (¹⁵· **i**   )
needed, and that's who he hired. And the employees themselves? They
(¹⁶· **l**   ) these jobs that give them a (¹⁷· **p**   ) in the world. Now
that's a real win-win.

E Discussion: Share your ideas and opinions with your classmates.

   1. Look for other stories about opportunities for people with special needs.
       Are you familiar with any programs in your area?
   2. People with special needs used to be referred to as "handicapped." What
       are more modern or polite ways to say the following?

             old person   overweight person   job loss

Useful Grammar from the News　② 話の連続性

　ニュース報道では，現地にいる人の生の声を紹介することがよくある。その場合，話の連続性を持たせるために，アンカーパーソンが，現地の人のことばを受けて，話のつながりをよくする工夫がされている。以下の例では，「自分の居場所がないような気がしていました。」と言うケリガンさんに対して，「今は（働く場所が）ありますね。」というように，アンカーパーソンが話をつなげている。

— *A. Kerrigan:* It makes me feel like there's not a place in me in this world.

— *D. Muir:* There is now, because Dallas businessman Tom Landis knew exactly the kind of workers he was looking for.

(No Limits Café, p.38)

— *D. Muir:* And what was her role?

— *Daughter:* The work was to take a Monroe or a Friden calculator...

(To the Moon, p.21)

— *D. Muir:* ...And when her daughter asked all those years later, what if someone questioned you?

— *Daughter:* What happened if somebody questioned your work?

(To the Moon, p.21)

— *K. Phillips:* The president today saying he believes the Taliban will abide by the deal. However...

— *D. Trump:* If bad things happen, we'll go back.　*(Ending the War?, p.50)*

Paralyzed Man Walks Again

Air Date: November 27, 2019
Duration: 2′ 13″

Before You Watch the News

Preview Questions

1. How did Chris Barr become paralyzed?

——クリス・バーさんが全身不随になった原因は何ですか。

2. How were the doctors able to treat him?

——医師はどのようにして彼を治療することができましたか。

Warm-up Exercises

A Vocabulary Check: Choose the correct definition for each of the words below.

1. groundbreaking　(　　)

2. prognosis　(　　)

3. plateau　(　　)

4. anxieties　(　　)

5. promote　(　　)

a. worries; concerns

b. the likely course of an illness or injury

c. pioneering; innovative

d. to advance or assist

e. to reach a state of no change after a period of progress

B Fill in the blanks with appropriate expressions from the Vocabulary
Check above. Change the word forms where necessary.

1. His doctor feels that with surgery, Grandpa's (　　　　　) is excellent.
2. Mari's French (　　　　　) for a while, but now she's improving
   dramatically with the new teacher.
3. The trial aims at (　　　　　) better sleeping habits in teens.
4. Mom started to see a counselor to help her deal with her (　　　　　).
5. The medical community has announced a (　　　　　) new drug to
   fight the virus.

News Story [2′ 13″]

T. Llamas: Finally tonight, "America
　　　Strong." A man paralyzed from the
　　　neck down, able to walk again
　　　thanks to a groundbreaking new
　　　treatment. Will Reeve is here with
　　　the remarkable and very personal
　　　story.

W. Reeve: Tonight, amateur surfer Chris Barr celebrating a milestone some
　　　might call miraculous. **1.** _____,
　　　Chris went head first into the ocean floor in northern California. The
　　　accident breaking his neck in eight places.

C. Barr: The prognosis was…was bad. Um, and bad meaning that, you know,
　　　probably a 95% to 97% chance that **2.** _____
　　　_____.

W. Reeve: So, lifetime of no movement.

C. Barr: Exactly.

W. Reeve: But with rehab, hope. **3.** _____,
　　　until he plateaued six months in and the recovery stopped. But then,
　　　Chris was accepted into an innovative trial led by Dr. Mohamad Bydon
　　　at the Mayo Clinic in Minnesota. Chris would be patient number one.

Patient number one?

C. Barr: Yeah.

W. Reeve: There's got to be some anxieties associated with that.

C. Barr, Wife: None.

C. Barr: You've got to understand: you've got absolutely nothing to lose.

W. Reeve: Dr. Bydon's team took stem cells from Chris's own stomach fat and injected them into his spinal cord to promote regeneration and recovery.

Dr. M. Bydon: After we treated him, 4. _____

_____.

C. Barr: It was fast. It was fast. I felt it going in. I felt it in my legs. I hadn't felt anything in my legs for... you know, for almost a year.

All right. You ready?

W. Reeve: Wow.

And we were there as Chris showed us first-hand what he once thought impossible. Walking again. On his own.

Does it feel good? Does it feel nice to just stand?

C. Barr: Yeah, it does. Ah...

W. Reeve: Never thought you'd do this again.

C. Barr: I'm telling you.

W. Reeve: You're standing and walking.

C. Barr: We're living it.

T. Llamas: Simply incredible. Will Reeve joins us now on set. The Mayo Clinic wanted to point out that Chris was a super responder.

W. Reeve: 5. _____. The Mayo Clinic did tell us that there are ten patients in this study, not all of them had Chris's response.

T. Llamas: Well, I'm curious. Your father was Christopher Reeve. What was it like to report on this story? Did you feel like [6.] _____ _____ ?

W. Reeve: I felt like I was witnessing the realization of my father's dream of a world of empty wheelchairs. 5

Notes **Will Reeve**「ウィル・リーブ〈ABC 放送のリポーター。父はスーパーマンを演じた俳優として有名な Christopher Reeve。ウィルさんが 3 歳になる前の 1995 年に，父は乗馬中に落馬し脊髄損傷を起こして首から下が麻痺した。その後は車椅子での生活を余儀なくされ 2004 年に亡くなった〉」 **milestone**「画期的な出来事；重要な意味を持つ出来事；大切な節目」 **rehab**「リハビリ〈rehabilitation〉」 **innovative trial**「革新的な治験（臨床試験）」 **the Mayo Clinic**「メイヨ・クリニック〈ミネソタ州ロチェスター市に本部を置く総合病院。クリニックという名称がついているが，大規模な病院〉」 **stem cells**「幹細胞〈様々な細胞に分化する能力を持つ特殊な細胞で，組織の再生などを担う〉」 **spinal cord**「脊髄」 **regeneration**「（神経などの）再生」 **first-hand**「本人からじかに（直接に）」 **I'm telling you.**「本当にその通りです」 **We're living it.**「大いに楽しんでいますよ」 **super responder**「（治療に対して）素晴らしく反応の良い人；素晴らしく病状が改善した人」

After You Watch the News

Exercises

A Listen to the CD and fill in the blanks in the text. ◎ CD 23

B Mark the following sentences true (T) or false (F) according to the information in the news story.

(   ) **1.** In spite of his negative prognosis, Chris Barr initially improved through rehabilitation.

(   ) **2.** Chris was willing to be the first patient in Dr. Bydon's groundbreaking trial.

(   ) **3.** The Mayo Clinic's innovative procedure involved injecting stem cells from healthy patients.

(   ) **4.** The clinic's new treatment has enabled 10 paralyzed patients to walk again.

(   ) **5.** After being paralyzed for a year, Chris began to recover quickly following the treatment.

(   ) **6.** Will Reeve's dream is to have a world of empty wheelchairs.

News Story 8 **45**

C Translate the following Japanese into English. Then listen to the CD and practice the conversation with your partner.

A: Is Chris really walking again? It's a miracle!

B: It sure is! ¹· <u>The doctors said</u> _____

_____ .

A: The rehabilitation really paid off.

B: It wasn't the rehab. ²· _____

<u>at the Mayo Clinic.</u>

A: I had no idea. He and his wife must have been pretty nervous.

B: ³· <u>Actually,</u> _____ .

A: He took a chance and now he's walking again. Wow!

1. 医者は95％の確率で全く動けなくなると言っていました。

2. 彼はメイヨ・クリニックの革新的な治験に参加していました。

3. 実際，クリスは失うものは何もないと思っていました。

D Summary Practice: Fill in the blanks with suitable words beginning with the letters indicated.

CD 25

When (¹· **a** _____) (²· **s** _____) Chris Barr broke his
(³· **n** _____) in eight places, leaving him (⁴· **p** _____), the
(⁵· **p** _____) was very bad. Three years later, his progress is
being called (⁶· **m** _____). (⁷· **R** _____) helped at first, but
(⁸· **p** _____) after just six months. Chris then entered an
(⁹· **i** _____) (¹⁰· **t** _____) at the Mayo Clinic as patient
number (¹¹· **o** _____). The (¹²· **g** _____) procedure
involved injecting (¹³· **s** _____) (¹⁴· **c** _____) from Chris's stomach fat into
his (¹⁵· **s** _____) cord to encourage recovery. According to Chris, the
(¹⁶· **i** _____) came fast. Now, incredibly, he is
standing and (¹⁷· **w** _____) on his own. The Mayo Clinic has called
Chris a (¹⁸· **s** _____) (¹⁹· **r** _____), adding that not all of the
(²⁰· **t** _____) patients in the trial did as well. According to Will Reeve,
watching Chris walk was like watching the (²¹· **r** _____) of
his dad's (²²· **d** _____) of a world of (²³· **e** _____) (²⁴· **w** _____).

46

E **Discussion: Share your ideas and opinions with your classmates.**

1. Chris Barr became paralyzed in a surfing accident. What are other causes of paralysis? See if you can find information about other treatments.

2. Look for other medical news stories. Share them with your classmates.

3. Christopher Reeve was the star of the *Superman* movies. Do an Internet search to find out more about the actor and the accident that left him paralyzed.

Pronunciation Hints from the News ① 聞こえなくなる音

　子音や母音が，口語体のくだけた発話において，聞こえなくなる現象を音声脱落（elision）現象という。話すスピードが速くなればなるほど，またカジュアルな場面での会話ほど音は脱落するか，はっきり発音されにくくなる。これは，発話速度が速くなると，それだけ発声器官の動きも速くなるため，出来るだけ調音運動を少なくしようとするからである。例えば，because の語頭音節が脱落した 'cause や，working の語尾を略した workin' のような表記は，歌の歌詞や映画のスクリプトなどでもよく見る。

　次の例の，months /mʌnθs/ では，語尾で /nθs/ のように子音が３つ連続している。この場合，/θ/ が脱落し，先行する /n/ と調音点が同じ /t/ に入れ替わって /mʌn(t)s/ と発音されるので「マンツ」のように聞こえる。同様に，clothes /kloʊðz/ のような語尾に子音が連続してくるときは，/ð/ が脱落して /kloʊz/ のように発音される。

— …, until he plateaued six ***months*** in and the recovery stopped.

(*Paralyzed Man Walks Again, p.43*)

— When the Salvation Army gives out the food and the ***clothes*** to the people in this area, … (*The Veteran and His Homemade Toys, p.14*)

Ending the War?

Air Date: February 29, 2020
Duration: 1' 57"

Before You Watch the News

Preview Questions

1. What war may be about to end?

——どの戦争が終わろうとしているのですか。

2. What are the conditions of the peace deal that was just signed?

——調印されたばかりの和平協定の条件は何ですか。

Warm-up Exercises

A Vocabulary Check: Choose the correct definition for each of the words below.

1. delegation (   )

2. pledge (   )

3. withdrawal (   )

4. commitment (   )

5. abide (   )

a. to obey; to follow

b. a group of representatives

c. to promise; to commit to

d. devotion; dedication

e. removal; ending

B **Fill in the blanks with appropriate expressions from the Vocabulary Check above. Change the word forms where necessary.**

1. Before joining the Scouts, we had to (   ) to obey the Girl Scout laws.
2. Lee is bright and he also has a strong sense of (   ). You should offer him the job.
3. If you can't (   ) by the rules, you'll be kicked out of the dorm.
4. The (   ) of aid from the refugees would lead to unimaginable problems.
5. A (   ) of faculty from our sister school in Canada is arriving next week.

News Story [1' 57"]

T. Llamas: The historic peace deal signed today that could finally bring an end to America's longest war. Secretary of State Mike Pompeo on hand in Doha, Qatar as the deal with the Taliban delegation was announced with the U.S. pledging to bring home U.S. troops if the Taliban meets certain conditions. So, 1. _____ and what are the chances it holds? ABC's Kyra Phillips is at the White House tonight.

K. Phillips: After nearly two trillion dollars and tens of thousands of lives, America's longest war may finally be nearing an end.

President D. Trump: We've had tremendous success in Afghanistan in the killing of terrorists but it's time, after all these years, to go and 2. _____ _____.

K. Phillips: The U.S. and Taliban agreeing that terrorist groups like Al Qaeda will not be allowed to operate in Afghanistan. In exchange, a timetable for the withdrawal of U.S. troops. Troops, the president says, 3. _____ _____.

Reporter: How soon do you expect troops to be coming back?

D. Trump: Um, like, uh, today.

K. Phillips: Some Republicans on Capitol Hill doubtful that the U.S. can trust the Taliban's commitment. But generals fighting the war *4.* _____. David spoke with the top U.S. commander in Afghanistan last February.

U.S. military commander: If neither side's gonna win it militarily, you have to move into a, towards a political settlement here.

D. Muir: Do you think those political talks with the Taliban are a key part of any end game here?

U.S. military commander: Absolutely.

K. Phillips: The president today saying he believes the Taliban will abide by the deal. However...

D. Trump: *5.* _____, we'll go back. I, let the people know, we'll go back and we'll go back so fast and we'll go back with a force like nobody's ever seen.

K. Phillips: Tom, the president also announcing he will be meeting with Taliban leaders in the, quote, "not so distant future." However, *6.* _____ _____, but you may remember, the last time he planned secret talks with Taliban leaders at Camp David, he cancelled.

5

10

15

20

Notes **peace deal**「和平協定；和平の取り決め」 **Secretary of State**「国務長官」 **on hand in ~**「~に来ている；~に来て（タリバン側との会合に）出席している」 **Doha**「ドーハ〈カタールの首都〉」 **Taliban**「タリバン〈アフガニスタンのイスラム原理主義組織。2000 年初頭，アフガニスタン国土の 9 割を支配していたと言われていたが，テロリストのオサマ・ビンラディンらをかくまったために，2001 年 10 月に米軍の攻撃が続き，タリバン政権は崩壊した。しかし，未だ残党（旧支配勢力）が活動している〉」 **Capitol Hill**「連邦議会〈キャピトル・ヒルは，ワシントン D.C. の連邦議事堂がある丘のことだが，議会そのものを指す〉 **generals**「将軍；司令官」 **end game**「最終局面；大詰め」 **Camp David**「キャンプ・デービッド〈メリーランド州の山地にある大統領の別荘で，外国要人との会談によく使われる〉」

タリバンはアフガニスタンで1996年に政権を握ったが、2001年9月の米同時多発テロを実行した国際テロ組織アルカイダ（Al Qaeda）をかくまったことから、アメリカの報復攻撃で政権を失った。しかし、混乱に乗じて再び広い地域を支配し、政府側部隊への攻撃は収まっていない。そのため米軍による旧支配勢力タリバンの戦闘員に対する攻撃は終わることなく2001年以来「アメリカ史上最長の戦争」（America's longest war）として続いている。

　2020年2月末にアメリカとタリバンは、アフガンからの米軍の14カ月以内の撤収（withdrawal）と、タリバンが国内でテロ組織の活動を許さないことを合意している。この和平協定（peace deal）には、アフガン政府とタリバンが停戦や将来の政治体制について協議を始めることも盛り込まれている。

　同協定には、アフガンに駐留中の約12,000人の米軍について、2020年7月中旬までに8,600人まで削減し、さらに2021年4月までに完全撤収することが明記された。トランプ米大統領は、撤収を急いで最終局面（end game）へ持ち込みたい考えである。その背景には、11月の大統領選で、米軍撤収を有権者へのアピール材料にしたいという思惑があったとされる。

　アフガニスタンの和平に向けたアメリカと旧支配勢力タリバンの合意署名から4カ月が過ぎた2020年7月3日付の『毎日新聞』によると、アフガン政府によるタリバンの捕虜解放が遅れており、政府とタリバンによる和平協定は実現していないという。依然として、タリバンとアフガン政府による戦闘は激しさを増しており、6月の1週間の間に政府軍の兵士ら291人が死亡した。

After　You Watch the News

Exercises

A Listen to the CD and fill in the blanks in the text.　CD 26

B Mark the following sentences true (T) or false (F) according to the information in the news story.

(   ) **1.** The historic peace treaty was signed by the U.S. Secretary of State and a Taliban delegation in Qatar.

(   ) **2.** The U.S. paid the Taliban nearly two trillion dollars to sign the peace deal.

(   ) **3.** The U.S. agreed to pull out all American troops on the condition that terrorist groups no longer be allowed to operate in Afghanistan.

(   ) **4.** Although some people doubt that the Taliban can be trusted, the U.S. president plans to begin withdrawing the troops immediately.

(   ) **5.** The top U.S. military leader does not believe that negotiating with the Taliban is worthwhile.

(   ) **6.** President Trump vowed that the U.S. will never return to Afghanistan.

C Translate the following Japanese into English. Then listen to the CD and practice the conversation with your partner.　　　　　　　 ⊙ CD 27

A: Did you hear the news? It looks like the war might finally be ending.

B: The war in Afghanistan? How can that be possible?

A: <u>¹. Mike Pompeo met with a Taliban delegation and _____</u>

_____.

B: It's great that the troops will finally be coming home, but isn't it risky?

A: <u>². Well, the Taliban agreed that _____</u>

_____.

B: <u>³. It's easy to say that, but _____</u>

_____?

A: With tens of thousands of lives lost, they have to try.

1. マイク・ポンペオがタリバンの代表団と会い，和平協定が実際に調印されました。

2. えー，タリバンは，アルカイダやその他のテロリストグループが国内で，もはや活動できなくなることで合意しました。

3. そう言うのは簡単ですが，アメリカは彼らの約束を本当に信用できるのでしょうか。

D Summary Practice: Fill in the blanks with suitable words beginning with the letters indicated.

CD 28

With the signing of a historic (¹· **p**   ) (²· **d**   ) today, the
(³· **w**   ) of American troops from (⁴· **A**   )
is expected to begin immediately, marking the end of America's
(⁵· **l**   ) war. Secretary of (⁶· **S**   ) Mike Pompeo traveled to
(⁷· **Q**   ) to meet with the Taliban (⁸· **d**   ), who
agreed to the conditions set forth by the U.S. The deal stated that
(⁹· **t**   ) groups like (¹⁰· **A**   ) (¹¹· **Q**   ) will no longer be
allowed to operate in Afghanistan. There is disagreement as to how much
the Taliban can be trusted to honor their (¹²· **c**   ),
but the top (¹³· **m**   ) (¹⁴· **c**   ) stated that
when neither side can win (¹⁵· **m**   ), only (¹⁶· **p**   )
talks can potentially lead to an (¹⁷· **e**   ) (¹⁸· **g**   ). President Trump
believes the Taliban will (¹⁹· **a**   ) by their commitment but if they do
not, he is prepared to go back with (²⁰· **f**   ).

E Discussion: Share your ideas and opinions with your classmates.

1. The agreement between the U.S. and the Taliban was signed at the end
   of February 2020. Do an Internet search for an update on this news story.
   What is the current situation between the U.S. and Afghanistan? Are
   there still American military personnel in the country?
2. How much do you know about Afghanistan? Choose any aspect of the
   country that interests you, such as geography, language, music or
   industry, and see what you can find out. Share your answers with your
   classmates.

　隣接する２つの音の一方が他方の音の影響を受けて，同じ音や似た音に変化したり，お互いに影響しあって別の音に変化したりする現象を同化（assimilation）という。この現象は単語内でも，単語間でも起こり，特に，隣接する子音どうしが影響を与えることで生まれる。自然な速さの発話でもしばしば起こるが，特に，ニュースの英語など話すスピードが速い時や，くだけた会話でよく見られる。

　以下の例の，bu**t y**ou という語の連鎖の場合，but の語尾子音 /t/ と you の語頭子音 /j/ が互いに影響をし合い，破擦音の /tʃ/ に変わる。そのために「バッチュ」のように聞こえる。

— …, ***but you*** may remember, the last time he planned secret talks with Taliban leaders at Camp David, he cancelled.

(Ending the War?, p.50)

　次の例では，di**d y**ou の did の語尾子音 /d/ と you の語頭子音 /j/ が互いに影響をし合い，破擦音の /dʒ/ に変わっている。そのために「ディジュ」のように聞こえる。

— ***Did you*** feel like…   *(Paralyzed Man Walks Again, p.45)*

— …, ***did you*** talk to the president at all about your decision regarding the recommendations?   *(Justice Department Turmoil, p.91)*

　また，以下の例の a**s y**ou は，「アズユ」ではなく，「アジュ」と聞こる。as /əz/ の語尾子音 /z/ と you の語頭子音 /j/ が互いに影響をし合い，摩擦音の /ʒ/ に変わっている。

— But ***as you***'re about to see tonight, when those loggers are then set free,…   *(Amazon on the Brink, p.56)*

News Story 10

Amazon on the Brink

Before **You Watch the News**

Air Date: February 18, 2020
Duration: 2′ 10″

Preview Questions

1. What is happening right now in the Amazon?
　——アマゾンで今，何が起きているのですか。

2. What are the causes of this problem?
　——この問題の原因は何ですか。

Warm-up Exercises

A **Vocabulary Check: Choose the correct definition for each of the words below.**

1. abundant　(　　)
2. ancestral　(　　)
3. raging　(　　)
4. federal　(　　)
5. ambush　(　　)

a. familial; inherited from ancestors
b. to attack by surprise
c. national
d. blazing; uncontrolled
e. plentiful

B Fill in the blanks with appropriate expressions from the Vocabulary Check above. Change the word forms where necessary.

1. We watched in horror as the old hotel was destroyed by a (   ) fire.

2. Authorities are trying to determine who (   ) a group of local farmers last week.

3. A new (   ) program aims to provide assistance to single mothers.

4. Although (   ) rainfall is expected throughout the spring, we could face a dry spell in the summer.

5. The whole family will return to their (   ) home for a week-long reunion.

News Story [2' 10"]

D. Muir: To the ABC News investigation, inside the Amazon rainforest. Amid a troubling new report, deforestation has more than doubled in January from just a year ago. But tonight, an indigenous tribe is fighting back, capturing illegal loggers themselves. But as you're about to see tonight, when those loggers are then set free, **1.** _____ _____. Here's ABC's Dan Harris and our team in the Amazon tonight.

D. Harris: Okay, so, they have a prisoner. He's got his hand on his pistol, another hand on a machete.

We're on the frontlines of a secret war.

We have no idea what we're getting into.

An indigenous tribe in the Amazon taking up arms, including rifles, knives, even bows and arrows, against illegal loggers **2.** _____. We're right there as members of a group that calls itself the Guardians of the Forest raid a camp of outlaw loggers.

Suspect: *(Speaking foreign language)*

D. Harris: "Oh, my God," says one suspect, "He's gonna kill me." All told, they captured seven loggers. There is abundant proof of the men's activities, even notes on ³· _____

_____.

This wood goes to local cattle ranchers, who build ah… fences around their area. And they're selling the stakes for those fences. And then it even shows right here how much money they're making.

L. Guajajara, leader, Guardians of the Forest: *(Speaking foreign language)*

D. Harris: The leader, whose name is Laercio Guajajara, lectures the suspects.

4. _____?

Suspect: *(Speaking foreign language)*

D. Harris: "Because," he says, "I don't have anything." Laercio says more than a third of his ancestral homeland has been destroyed. Scientists now worry that the Amazon may be at a tipping point. After raging fires and an increase in illegal logging, deforestation doubled in January compared to last year. After forcing the loggers to burn down their own camp, Laercio's group brings them to Brazil's federal police. ⁵· _____

_____, Laercio is ambushed and shot by loggers, his deputy killed. This, he tells us, represents the beginning of a war.

Notes **deforestation**「森林破壊」 **indigenous tribe**「地元の（先住）部族（民族）」 **deadly force**「殺傷能力のある武器」 **prisoner**「拘束されている違法森林伐採者」 **machete**「ナタ〈中南米で現地住民が使用する長刀のナタ〉」 **Guardians of the Forest**「森の番人」 **cattle ranchers**「牛の牧場主（牧場経営者）」 **stakes**「杭」 **tipping point**「（重大な変化が起きる）転換点」 **deputy**「サブリーダー」

Background of the News

　南米アマゾン川流域の熱帯雨林（rainforest）は，世界の原生林の約3分の1を占める。森林が二酸化炭素を吸収し酸素を供給する働きから「地球の肺」として知られている。この約550万平方キロの広大な熱帯雨林は，コロンビア，ペルーなど9カ国にまたがり，その約6割がブラジルにある。ブラジルでは，環境保護より開発を優先するボルソナロ大統領が2019年1月に就任して以降，アマゾンの熱帯雨林の破壊が深刻化している。

　2020年6月27日付の『日本経済新聞』によると，新型コロナウイルスの感染拡大により警備が手薄となるなか，伐採面積は前年同期を3割超えるペースで広がっているという。アマゾンでは（重大な変化が起きる）転換点（tipping point）を迎えており，熱帯雨林の20％近い面積が失われたとする研究者の試算もある。

After | You Watch the News

Exercises

A Listen to the CD and fill in the blanks in the text.　　　CD 29

B Multiple Choice Questions

　1. What are the two sides in the "secret war"?
　　a. an indigenous tribe vs. the Guardians of the Forest
　　b. the Guardians of the Forest vs. the illegal loggers
　　c. the loggers vs. Brazil's federal police

　2. Which of the following is *NOT* a reason for deforestation of the Amazon?
　　a. wildfires
　　b. an increase in illegal logging
　　c. sale of the land to local cattle ranchers

　3. The seven captured loggers
　　a. were ambushed and then shot, and one of them died.
　　b. burned down their own camp and were brought to the police.
　　c. had been earning money by building fences for cattle ranchers.

4. Laercio Guajajara and his group

    a. have seen a large portion of their homeland destroyed.

    b. are now being protected by Brazil's federal police.

    c. are going after the ranchers in order to protect the rainforest.

C **Translate the following Japanese into English. Then listen to the CD and practice the conversation with your partner.** ◎ CD 30

A: ¹· <u>I just read that</u> _____

_____.

B: The wildfires have been out of control.

A: It's not just the fires. Illegal loggers are chopping down the trees and selling the wood.

B: Who would buy it? Don't people care about deforestation?

A: Not the cattle ranchers. ²·_____

_____.

B: But what does that mean for the indigenous tribes who live in the forest?

A: They're fighting back! ³· <u>It said</u> _____

_____.

1. アマゾンの熱帯雨林の森林破壊が２倍以上になっていると読んだばかりです。

2. 彼らは伐採者から杭を買ってフェンスを作っています。

3. ７人の無法者の伐採者たちを捕まえて警察に連行したと書いてありました。

D Summary Practice: Fill in the blanks with suitable words beginning with the letters indicated.

CD 31

Dan Harris and his ABC (¹· t _____) went to the (²· A _____) to report on (³· d _____) of the (⁴· r _____), which more than (⁵· d _____) in just a year. An (⁶· i _____) tribe has decided to go after (⁷· i _____) (⁸· l _____) because of the destruction of over one third of their (⁹· a _____) home. Armed with (¹⁰· r _____), knives, (¹¹· b _____) and (¹²· a _____), the indigenous (¹³· G _____) of the Forest are determined to (¹⁴· p _____) their land from the loggers who are cutting down (¹⁵· t _____) to supply the local (¹⁶· c _____) (¹⁷· r _____). Group (¹⁸· l _____) Laercio Guajajara found (¹⁹· a _____) proof of the loggers' illegal activities. His group forced them to (²⁰· b _____) down their (²¹· c _____) and turned them over to the (²²· p _____). That, however, triggered a violent reaction that led to Laercio being (²³· a _____) and shot—acts which he believes could start a (²⁴· w _____).

E Discussion: Share your ideas and opinions with your classmates.

1. Deforestation in the Amazon rainforest has been an ongoing environmental crisis. Look for an update on the problem of illegal logging. How is the Brazilian government dealing with these problems?

2. How much do you know about the indigenous tribes in the Amazon? How many tribes are there? Do an Internet search to see what you can learn about their languages and way of life.

News Story 11

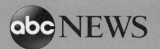

Emergency Business Aid

Before **You Watch the News**

Air Date: April 22, 2020
Duration: 1' 58"

Preview Questions

1. What is the situation of many small businesses in the U.S. right now?
   ——アメリカの多くの中小企業は今，どのような状況にあるのでしょうか。

2. Why are some of them complaining?
   ——不平を述べている人がいるのはなぜですか。

Warm-up Exercises

A **Vocabulary Check: Choose the correct definition for each of the words below.**

1. lay off (   )
2. rely on (   )
3. livelihood (   )
4. outrage (   )
5. impact (   )

a. source of income; means of support
b. anger; shock
c. to have a strong effect on; to influence
d. to fire; to let go
e. to count on; to depend on

61

B Fill in the blanks with appropriate expressions from the Vocabulary Check above. Change the word forms where necessary.

1. Don't worry about finding a new apartment. You can (   ) Jeff to help.
2. The airline may have to (   ) more pilots if the strike continues.
3. The harsh winter has negatively (   ) consumer spending.
4. There are many people whose (   ) depend on those crops.
5. Many fans reacted with (   ) when they learned the concert was cancelled.

News Story [1' 58"]

D. Muir: Small businesses in this country waiting for that news today, owners trying to save their businesses and really save their workers. Here's ABC's Steve Osunsami.

5

S. Osunsami: Business owner Mary Moore in Atlanta…

M. Moore, CEO, The Cook's Warehouse: Welcome to The Cook's Warehouse.

S. Osunsami: …says ¹._____ to keep 12 of her best people on the payroll. She's already had to lay off 43.

10

M. Moore: They rely on this business for their livelihoods, and I rely on them.

S. Osunsami: She owns The Cook's Warehouse stores and is trying to make the best of sales online. She's applied for government loans, but hasn't seen the final paperwork, and says the program is ². _____
_____.

15

M. Moore: It's really difficult as a small business person to hear how big corporations are getting grants and they're being given money. But I've got this great opportunity to create more debt for my business that, you know, I have to figure out ³. _____
_____.

20

S. Osunsami: An Associated Press investigation tonight speaks to this, finding that of the $349 billion in relief meant for small businesses, at least 75 companies that were helped are so big that they're publicly traded and some had market values greater than $100 million. Big chains like Ruth's Chris got money before the pot ran out last week. Shake Shack,

4. _____, gave $10 million back to the government after the outrage. As for that $384 billion in new help for small businesses? At Ben's Chili Bowl, a local institution in the nation's capital, they're still worried.

S. Ali, Co-owner, Ben's Chili Bowl: When we reopen, are we able to seat 50 or 60 or 70 people when you have to have **5.** _____

_____, etcetera? So, it impacts the entire business all the way around.

S. Osunsami: Nearly half the nation's workforce gets a paycheck from small businesses like these.

This time, the money meant for small businesses should be spent a little differently. About $60 billion has been set aside for these small businesses **6.** _____. But there is general agreement that this money still may not be enough.

Notes **Atlanta**「アトランタ〈ジョージア州北西部の都市で州都〉」 **keep ~ on the payroll**「~を継続して雇う」 **make the best of ~**「(不利な状況で) ~を最大限に活用する;~をフル活用する」 **government loans**「政府による融資」 **grants**「補助金」 **Associated Press investigation**「AP 通信社の調査〈AP はアメリカ最大の通信社〉」 **publicly traded**「株式公開されている;(証券取引所) に上場している」 **Ruth's Chris**「ルース・クリス (ステーキハウス)〈アメリカの高級ステーキハウスチェーン店〉」 **pot**「政府融資の資金 (全体の予算額)」 **Shake Shack**「シェイク・シャック〈ニューヨークに本社を置く大手ハンバーガーチェーン店〉」 **all the way around**「(ビジネス) 全般」 **has been set aside for ~**「~のために確保されている」

Background of the News

新型コロナウイルスの感染者数が世界一のアメリカ（2020年9月25日現在，感染者数約697万人）では，経済活動の停滞が深刻化し，特に中小企業（small businesses）の経営を圧迫している。2020年3月に成立した大型経済政策で，米政府は，従業員500人以下の中小企業を対象とした資金繰り支援策を実施した。雇用を維持する（keep people on the payroll）ため，3,490億ドルの政府融資（government loans）を従業員の給与支払いに充てれば返済を不要にする制度である。

2020年4月23日付の『日本経済新聞』によると，2020年4月初旬から始まったこの政府融資の受け付けに申請が殺到したため，わずか2週間で資金が枯渇したという。政府は4月24日に3,840億ドルの追加対策を決めたが，100万社以上の企業は支援が決まらない状態が続いた。本ニュースストーリーの冒頭に「そのニュースを待っていた（waiting for that news）」と出てくるが，この追加支援政策のことを指している。

本来，これは中小企業向けの融資ではあるが，大企業シェイク・シャック（Shake Shack）も融資を受けることができた。チェーン店の場合，店舗ごとで500人以下の要件を満たせばよい。同社はアメリカで8,000人規模の雇用を抱えるが，1店舗あたりの人員は45人程度なので，支援の対象になった。そのため，中小企業経営者から不公平（unfair）という怒りの声（outrage）が高まり，同社は補助金を全額返納した。

After You Watch the News

Exercises

A Listen to the CD and fill in the blanks in the text.　　　　◎ CD 32

B Multiple Choice Questions

1. Small business owners are struggling because
    a. they are expected to give money back to the government.
    b. their employees are expecting to be paid even if they cannot work.
    c. they are not getting the money that they expected from the government.

2. Mary Moore is worried that
    a. she will have to lay off even more of her employees.
    b. she will not be able to get good people to work for her.
    c. moving her business online will make her ineligible for relief money.

3. An Associated Press investigation found that
   a. many small businesses are unfairly getting more money than they should.
   b. 75% of the companies that received relief money are in fact large, publicly traded businesses.
   c. distribution of the $349 billion in relief aid for small businesses has not been fair.

4. According to the news story
   a. a special fund is being made available for small businesses that reopen.
   b. almost 50% of Americans earn their livelihoods from small businesses.
   c. small business owners are confident that they will finally get the financial support they need to stay open.

C **Translate the following Japanese into English. Then listen to the CD and practice the conversation with your partner.** ⊚ CD 33

A: Mary, you look upset. More bad news? ¹· _____
_____?

B: No, Jon. Not yet—but I am pretty worried.

A: ²· _____
_____?

B: I sure hope so. Nothing is finalized yet, though.

A: How can big chains like Shake Shack be getting relief funds, and not us?

B: It's so unfair. ³· _____
_____, but we need the help.

A: Well, in the meantime, let's keep pushing those online sales.

1. 私は解雇されるのですか。
2. もうすぐ政府から例の融資が受けられるのですよね。
3. 12人しか従業員が残っていないけれど，支援が必要なのです。

D Summary Practice: Fill in the blanks with suitable words beginning with the letters indicated.

🔘 CD 34

Mary Moore, (¹· o _____) of The Cook's (²· W _____) stores, is one of many small business owners across the U.S. struggling to save their businesses and their (³· w _____). Having already (⁴· l _____) (⁵· o _____) 43 employees, Mary is intent on keeping her (⁶· t _____) best workers, aware that their (⁷· l _____) depend on it. At Ben's Chili Bowl, an (⁸· i _____) in the nation's (⁹· c _____), the co-owner is voicing similar concerns.

What is the government doing? (¹⁰· L _____) and grants are being made available, but of the $349 (¹¹· b _____) intended to help (¹²· s _____) businesses, an (¹³· i _____) by the Associated Press has determined that at least (¹⁴· s _____)-(¹⁵· f _____) big chains like Ruth's Chris received big chunks of financial assistance. Popular (¹⁶· S _____) (¹⁷· S _____) in fact returned $10 million to the government following public (¹⁸· o _____). Another round of financial support is set to be released, but small business owners worry that it may not be enough to support the businesses that provide (¹⁹· p _____) to nearly (²⁰· h _____) of all Americans.

E Discussion: Share your ideas and opinions with your classmates.

1. What kinds of support, financial and otherwise, did the Japanese government make available during the coronavirus pandemic? Was there any special assistance given to small businesses?

2. Choose another country and do an Internet search to find out what kinds of support were provided to individuals and businesses during the pandemic. Share the information with your classmates.

3. In what ways did the economic problems during this period affect your community? Are you aware of any local restaurants or other businesses that had to close? Do you know of any businesses that shifted their business online?

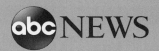

Classic American Cowboy Hat

MADE IN AMERICA

Before You Watch the News

Air Date: September 13, 2019
Duration: 2′ 21″

Preview Questions

1. How long have cowboy hats been made in the U.S.?

——アメリカではいつからカウボーイハットが作られているのですか。

2. Why are the workers that make Stetson hats so proud?

——ステットソンハットを作る労働者は，なぜ誇りを持っているのですか。

Warm-up Exercises

A Vocabulary Check: Choose the correct definition for each of the words below.

1. inadequate ( )

2. get by ( )

3. decade ( )

4. underdressed ( )

5. snug ( )

a. tight; close-fitting

b. a period of ten years

c. dressed too informally

d. gain approval

e. insufficient; not good enough

B Fill in the blanks with appropriate expressions from the Vocabulary Check above. Change the word forms where necessary.

1. That skirt looks a bit (   ). Why don't you try a larger size?

2. I thought my essay was (   ), but I got an "A."

3. Everybody showed up in a suit! I felt so (   ) in jeans.

4. A new vending machine? That will never (   ) the budget committee.

5. Gus and Jan have been going out for a (   ). Do you think they'll ever get married?

News Story [2′ 21″]

D. Muir: Finally tonight here, "Made in America" is back. And you already know that, wherever we go, we like to find something made in America. So, while in Texas this week, we found a true American original.

5

1. _____

and the country. And we set out to find them, an American classic, a Stetson hat.

10

J. Thomason, quality control manager, Stetson: Hello, sir, how are you?

D. Muir: I can tell by the hats.

Founded by John B. Stetson, 1865, during the Gold Rush.

He traveled out west.

A. Bozeman, senior VP, marketing & e-commerce, Stetson: He did.

15

D. Muir: *2.* _____ like everybody else?

A. Bozeman: He was. He… ah set out to Pikes Peak and, on his way, uhm, realized that people had inadequate headwear.

D. Muir: At the time, selling hats for $5. And by 1900, he had the largest hat factory in the world. And more than a century later, in Garland, Texas, more than 200 workers at their factory. They make one million hats every year. And those

hats have to get by this guy, Justin Thomason, head of quality control

3. _____.

I have to admit—I'm feeling a little underdressed here.

J. Thomason: You should be. You're in Texas, you need a hat.

D. Muir: I definitely need—I need a Stetson.

Justin proud to show me the label inside.

And you can see right here, it says, uh, made in the USA.

J. Thomason: Yes.

D. Muir: And 4. _____?

J. Thomason: Absolutely.

D. Muir: And behind every Stetson hat, a long line of proud American workers.

How many people do you think went into shaping and making this hat?

J. Thomason: Ahm... there's about 100 sets of hands...

D. Muir: No kidding?

J. Thomason: ...that touched that hat.

D. Muir: On every hat?

J. Thomason: Yes.

D. Muir: They made hats for Buffalo Bill, Will Rogers, Annie Oakley, James Dean, Roy Rogers, Ronald Reagan, and Indiana Jones. And 5. _____ _____ to find the right fit for me.

All right, let's give it a shot.

J. Thomason: All right, that looks really good.

D. Muir: Yeah?

J. Thomason: Yes.

D. Muir: What do you think?   5

J. Thomason: You just want just a little snug on the front of your forehead...

D. Muir: Yeah?

J. Thomason: ...to where it's not gonna blow away. It looks really good.

D. Muir: Yeah. You think I can pull it off?

J. Thomason: Absolutely. You're doing it right now.   10

D. Muir: All right, well.

J. Thomason: I think ^{6.} _____.

D. Muir: We'll let everybody at home decide that.

J. Thomason: Ha ha ha...

D. Muir: Tonight, in that Texas factory, a tip of the hat to those workers. Many   15
of their families there for generations.

Employee: We're proud of that fact. And we actually sticker the boxes, Made
in USA.

D. Muir: ^{7.} _____. And all of us love a good
Stetson.   20

Employees: Made in America.

D. Muir: We love "Made in America." And thank you for watching here on a
Friday night. I'm David Muir. Hope to see you right back here on
Monday. Good night.

Notes　**Stetson hat**「ステットソンハット」　**quality control manager**「品質管理責任者」　**Gold Rush**「ゴールドラッシュ（時代）〈1800 年代半ば，アメリカ西部での金鉱の発見による大規模で急速な人口の移動〉」　**senior VP, marketing & e-commerce**「マーケティング及び e コマース担当上級副社長」　**Pikes Peak**「パイクスピーク〈ロッキー山脈にある山で，現在はリゾート地〉」　**Garland**「ガーランド〈テキサス州，ダラス北東方向に位置する都市〉」　**Buffalo Bill**「バッファロー・ビル〈1868 年のバッファロー狩りコンテストで優勝した軍人・開拓者の William Frederick Cody（1846-1917）につけられたニックネーム〉」　**Will Rogers**「ウィル・ロジャース〈チェロキー族の血を受けたカウボーイ，コメディアン，俳優（1879 ～ 1935 年）〉」　**Annie Oakley**「アニー・オークレー〈射撃の名人でバッファロー・ビルのワイルド・ウエスト・ショーで働いた。映画 *Annie Get Your Gun*（1950 年）のモデル（1860 ～ 1926 年）」　**James Dean**「ジェームズ・ディーン〈「エデンの東」（1955 年），「理由なき反抗」（1955 年），「ジャイアンツ」（1956 年）などに主演した俳優（1931 ～ 1955 年）〉」　**Roy Rogers**「ロイ・ロジャース〈歌手, 俳優, テレビ司会者で「カウボーイの王様」として知られていた（1911 ～ 1998 年）〉」　**Ronald Reagan**「ロナルド・レーガン〈第 40 代アメリカ大統領（1981 ～ 1989 年）俳優から政治の道へ進んだ（1911 ～ 2004 年）〉」　**Indiana Jones**「インディアナ・ジョーンズ〈映画「レイダース／失われたアーク《聖櫃》（*Raiders of the Lost Ark*）」の主人公でカウボーイハットがトレードマーク。ハリソン・フォードが演じた〉」　**give it a shot**「試してみる；試着する」　**pull it off**「着こなす；似合う」　**tip of the hat**「敬意」

After　You Watch the News

Exercises

A Listen to the CD and fill in the blanks in the text.　◉ CD 35

B Multiple Choice Questions

1. John B. Stetson traveled out west in order to
   a. search for gold.
   b. sell a new kind of hat.
   c. search for material for a new kind of hat.

2. In the year 1900, Stetson
   a. had 200 workers in his factory.
   b. had the largest hat factory in the world.
   c. sold one million hats that year for $5 each.

3. Which of the following is *NOT* true about Stetson hats?
   a. They should fit the head snugly.
   b. They were worn by many famous Americans.
   c. They are made by members of the extended Stetson family.

4. Each Stetson hat

    a. has a "Made in Texas" sticker inside.

    b. has to be approved by Justin Thomason.

    c. was made by a team of 50 factory workers.

C **Translate the following Japanese into English. Then listen to the CD and practice the conversation with your partner.**   ◎ CD 36

A: How was your trip to Texas, Tony?

B: I had a fantastic time! And I got you a souvenir. Open the box.

A: Wow! ¹·_____!

B: Try it on. Let's see how you look.

A: ²· _____.

B: That's exactly how it's supposed to fit. ³· _____!

A: I love it, Tony. And it was made in America!

1. ステットソンの帽子がずっと欲しかったんだ。

2. おでこの前が少しきついかな。

3. まるで本物のテキサス州人みたいだよ。

D **Summary Practice: Fill in the blanks with suitable words beginning with the letters indicated.**   ◎ CD 37

David Muir traveled to (¹· **T**   ) where his search for products "Made in America" turned up a real (²· **A**   ) (³· **c**   ): Stetson hats. The (⁴· **c**   ) hats date back to the days of the (⁵· **G**   ) (⁶· **R**   ), when John B. Stetson, headed for (⁷· **P**   ) (⁸· **P**   ), noticed a problem of (⁹· **i**   ) headwear among people searching for gold. By 1900 his hat (¹⁰· **f**   ) was the biggest one in the world. A century later, the (¹¹· **t**   ) (¹²· **h**   ) employees at their Texas factory make a (¹³· **m**   ) of the distinctive hats each year. One hundred (¹⁴· **w**   ) are involved in the making of each hat, with the final product approved by the head of (¹⁵· **q**   ) (¹⁶· **c**   ), Justin Thomason. Over the years, Stetson hats have been made for (¹⁷· **J**   ) (¹⁸· **D**   ), Ronald Reagan and even (¹⁹· **I**   ) (²⁰· **J**   )! And now David Muir will proudly wear one, too—if he can pull it off.

E Discussion: Share your ideas and opinions with your classmates.

1. The history of Stetson hats dates back to the time of the Gold Rush. Do an Internet search to see what you can find out about that period of American history.

2. Cowboy hats, and especially authentic Stetsons, are considered to be 100% American. Are there any kinds of clothing that are strongly affiliated with Japan? Are there any special bags or articles of clothing manufactured in your town?

　ニュースでは，親しみやすさを示すために，口語的なイディオムがよく使用される。ステットソンハットについてリポートしたこのニュースストーリーでは，以下のようなハットにまつわるイディオムを利用した軽快な「ことば遊び」が見られる。

— Tonight, in that Texas factory, ***a tip of the hat*** to those workers.
(Classic American Cowboy Hat, p.70)

　tip one's hat to ~ は，「帽子を取って（軽く持ち上げ）人に挨拶する（敬意；謝意を表す）」という意味で，名詞としての a tip of the hat は「感謝の（敬意を示す）言葉」という意味になる。

　以下の例では，デイトナ500カーレースを訪問したトランプ大統領がレースコースを専用車で周回して群衆を「熱狂させた」ことが紹介されている。rev up で「エンジンの回転数を上げる」という意味があり，一種の「かけことば」になっている。

— President Trump in Florida today, ***revvin' up*** the crowd as grand
　marshal at the Daytona 500.　　　*(Justice Department Turmoil, p.91)*

　また，前置詞を含むイディオムや句動詞を使うことで，ニュースに軽快できびきびとした印象を与える。イディオムは一気に発音されるので，ニュースに音声的なリズムも生まれる。

— But the plan ***backs off of*** the more sweeping changes President
　Trump first proposed.　　　*(E-Cigarette: Partial Ban Backlash, p.7)*
— Secretary of State Mike Pompeo ***on hand in*** Doha,...
(Ending the War?, p.49)
— ***Taking a lap*** in his limo, the Beast, before thousands of NASCAR
　super fans.　　　*(Justice Department Turmoil, p.91)*
— It was ***thrown out***, prompting all four prosecutors on the case to
　resign.　　　*(Justice Department Turmoil, p.92)*

Anger Across America

Air Date: June 3, 2020
Duration: 2′ 29″

Before You Watch the News

Preview Questions

1. Why are people protesting across the U.S.?

——なぜ全米で抗議行動が起きているのですか。

2. What was the message from former President Obama?

——オバマ前大統領からは，どのようなメッセージが送られましたか。

Warm-up Exercises

A **Vocabulary Check: Choose the correct definition for each of the words below.**

1. brutality (　　)

2. urge (　　)

3. controversial (　　)

4. tactic (　　)

5. vow (　　)

a. strategy; course of action

b. to promise

c. to try to persuade someone to do something

d. debatable; likely to trigger strong feelings, both pro and con

e. physical violence

B **Fill in the blanks with appropriate expressions from the Vocabulary Check above. Change the word forms where necessary.**

1. The students were (   ) to find housing close to campus.
2. Kim (   ) to keep my secret, but she told three other friends.
3. Delaying the election is not a smart (   ) if you feel confident of winning.
4. We liked the film, but it showed too much (   ).
5. The mayor's plan for the new building is still (   ).

News Story [2′ 29″]

D. Muir: Protesters are taking to the streets across America tonight for a ninth day now, expressing anger, but also hope. And tonight, we hear what they have to say after learning that the other officers have now been charged. And the message late today for young men and women of color in this country from President Obama, saying, "I want you to know that your lives matter." ABC's Stephanie Ramos here in New York.

S. Ramos: ¹._____ since the killing of George Floyd. Thousands protesting racism and police brutality.

Protesters, group: Hands up. Don't shoot.

S. Ramos: Calling for charges for all of the officers involved. Tonight, word reaching protesters.

What do you think about the charges that the officers... former officers are now facing?

Protester 1: Now! Now! It took protests, it took cities burning for you to arrest four people.

Protester 2: I'm so happy. I... I still think it's not enough, but I'm so happy that [2.] _____

_____

because, a few years ago, I don't think this would have happened.

S. Ramos: Large crowds turning out today from New York, to Los Angeles, to the U.S. capital, where protesters lied face down in silence in remembrance of George Floyd.

Protesters, group: Take a knee. Take a knee.

S. Ramos: The crowd urging Capitol Police to take a knee. For days, protesters in Philadelphia [3.] _____ this controversial statue of former mayor and police commissioner Frank Rizzo, widely accused of being a symbol of racism for his tactics against the black community in the 1960s and '70s. The city taking it down in the middle of the night.

Mayor J. Kenney, Philadelphia, Pennsylvania: This is the beginning of the healing process in our city. This is not the end. [4.] _____

_____.

S. Ramos: As word of those new charges reached George Floyd's brother in New York, he joined New York's police commissioner, vowing to press for change.

T. Floyd, brother of George Floyd: We're moving in the direction of justice, and that's a good thing. But [5.] _____

_____.

S. Ramos: Late today, former President Barack Obama making his first on-camera comments about George Floyd and the protests.

Former President B. Obama: You've communicated a sense of urgency that is as powerful and as transformative as anything that I've seen, uh, in recent years.

S. Ramos: At this point, David, protesters tell me they have no intention of stopping these demonstrations. They have told me every single day that

they just want racism to end. They call the charges against the officers today a step, *6.* _____,
David.

D. Muir: Stephanie Ramos in New York again tonight. Stephanie, thank you.

Notes　　**Hands up. Don't shoot.**「手を挙げているのだから，撃たないで。〈2014 年 8 月，ミズーリ州ファーガソンで武器を所持していない 18 歳のアフリカ系アメリカ人の少年が，"Hands up. Don't shoot." と訴えたにもかかわらず，警察によって射殺された事件に基づいている〉」　**word**「情報〈この意味の場合は不可算名詞〉」　**turning out**「集まる；集結する」　**lied**「横たわった〈文法的には lay が正しい〉」　**in remembrance of ~**「～を追悼して；を偲んで」　**Take a knee.**「ひざまづけ〈人種差別に異議を唱えるため NFL（米フットボールリーグ）の選手が始めた片ひざをつくポーズ〉」　**Capitol Police**「（合衆国）議会警察〈=United States Capitol Police〉」　**police commissioner**「警察本部長」　**Frank Rizzo**「フランク・リゾ〈60 ～ 70 年代にアフリカ系アメリカ人や性的少数者を弾圧した〉」　**healing process**「（痛手から）立ち直る過程」　**press for ~**「～を強く求める；～を要求する」　**on-camera**「収録動画の」　**sense of urgency**「緊迫感」　**transformative**「改革的；変革を起こす勢いがある」

Background of the News

　アメリカでは建国以来，黒人差別の歴史がある。マーチン・ルーサー・キング牧師が黒人差別撤廃を訴え，1963 年には，20 万人以上が参加した「ワシントン大行進」が行われた。それが 1964 年の人種差別（racism）を禁じる「公民権法」の成立につながったが，差別は完全にはなくならず，今回のような警官による黒人への虐待行為が度々問題になっている。

　1992 年には，ロサンゼルスで黒人青年に暴行した警官への無罪評決をきっかけに暴動が起こり，大規模な「ロサンゼルス暴動」が発生した。また，2012 年には，フロリダ州で黒人の少年が自警団の白人男性に射殺され，翌年には無罪評決が出たことで全米に抗議運動が広がった。この時，「黒人の命は大切だ」（Black Lives Matter）がスローガンになった。さらに，2014 年 7 月，ニューヨークで警官に腕で首を絞められた黒人男性が「息ができない」（I can't breathe.）と何度も訴えながら死亡した。

　2020 年 5 月 25 日，偽造紙幣を使った疑いで，警官が路上でジョージ・フロイドさんに手錠をかけて拘束した。うつぶせになったフロイドさんの首を膝で 9 分間近く押さえ付け，意識を失った後も 3 分ほど続けたため，搬送先の病院で死亡した。フロイドさんも「息ができない」（I can't breathe.）などと悲痛に訴え続け，助けを求めていたという。

　この事件を発端に，全米各地で暴動が起き，6 月に入っても抗議デモ（protest）が続いた。2020 年 6 月 2 日付の『毎日新聞』によると，首都ワシントンと 15 の州に州兵計約 5,000 人が動員され，全米約 40 都市で夜間外出禁止令が出された。これだけの規模の夜間外出禁止令は，キング牧師が 1968 年に暗殺されて以来だという。ミネソタ州の司法当局は 6 月 3 日，関与した元警察官（former officers）4 人全員を訴追した。

After | You Watch the News

Exercises

A Listen to the CD and fill in the blanks in the text.

B Multiple Choice Questions

1. Which of the following did *NOT* occur on the day of the news broadcast?
   a. Protesters marched for the ninth day in a row in remembrance of George Floyd.
   b. George Floyd's brother met with Barack Obama to talk about racial injustice.
   c. Barack Obama spoke to young African Americans assuring them that their lives matter.

2. The protesters
   a. were critical of the current mayor of Philadelphia.
   b. urged police officers in the U.S. capital to take a knee.
   c. successfully tore down the statue of a controversial former mayor.

3. The brother of George Floyd
   a. expressed anger at the New York police commissioner.
   b. expressed happiness that his brother's death is leading to change.
   c. expressed hope and his belief in the need to keep fighting for justice.

4. Former President Obama
   a. praised the protesters for the sense of urgency in their fight.
   b. honored the protesters for finding peaceful ways to protest racism.
   c. encouraged the protesters to continue their fight with more urgency.

C Translate the following Japanese into English. Then listen to the CD and practice the conversation with your partner. ◉ CD 39

A: Where are you going now?

B: There's another protest. We're expecting thousands to show up.

A: ¹. _____.

  Why are you still protesting?

B: Don't you get it? This is just the beginning.

A: ². _____

  _____. How long is it going to go on?

B: For as long as it takes! ³. _____

_____.

A: You're right. Okay, let me get my bag. I'm going with you.

1. でも，警官はみんな起訴されたのです。

2. これで，あなたは９日連続で参加しているのですよ。

3. 人種差別と警察の横暴は，この国の大きな問題です。

D Summary Practice: Fill in the blanks with suitable words beginning with the letters indicated. ◉ CD 40

Anger and (¹· **h**   ) were the prevailing sentiments as protesters took to the streets for a (²· **n**   ) day of protests following the death of George Floyd. From (³· **N**   ) (⁴· **Y**   ) to L.A., in cities all across the country, thousands of protesters are calling for an end to (⁵· **r**   ) and police (⁶· **b**   ). With word that the other officers present at Floyd's killing have also been officially (⁷· **c**   ), some voiced anger and others, hope that change is finally coming. In the nation's (⁸· **c**   ), protesters lay face down in (⁹· **s**   ) as they remembered George Floyd. Meanwhile, in Philadelphia, a controversial statue of (¹⁰· **F**   ) (¹¹· **R**   ) was removed in the (¹²· **m**   ) of the night. Rizzo was a former mayor and police commissioner who was a (¹³· **s**   ) of racism during the 1960s and '70s. George Floyd's (¹⁴· **b**   ) and (¹⁵· **f**   ) President Barack Obama expressed support for the protesters, acknowledging that there is now hope for (¹⁶· **j**   ). The protesters themselves plan to continue the (¹⁷· **d**   ), which they hope will finally bring an end to racism.

E Discussion: Share your ideas and opinions with your classmates.

1. How much do you know about races in the U.S.? What percentage of the population is African American? The Black Lives Matter movement, promoting non-violent protest against racially motivated violence against Black people, was founded in 2013. See what you can find out about the movement.

2. The three people listed below all had a big impact on the lives of African Americans. Choose one of them and do an Internet search to find more information about their influence on race relations in the U.S. Share your findings with your classmates.

      Rosa Parks   John Lewis   Barack Obama

3. In addition to police brutality and race relations, young Americans have also been actively protesting gun laws and other issues in the U.S. Are young Japanese politically active? What are some causes that they have recently supported? Do they often participate in protests?

Volunteers Feeding Those in Need

EMERGENCY ENTRANCE ONLY

Before You Watch the News

Air Date: April 10, 2020
Duration: 2' 33"

Preview Questions

1. What kind of new volunteer groups have been started in the U.S.?
   ——アメリカではどのような新しいボランティア団体が始まっているのですか。

2. Who do they aim to help?
   ——誰を助けることを目的としているのですか。

Warm-up Exercises

A Vocabulary Check: Choose the correct definition for each of the words below.

1. generosity (　　)
2. relief (　　)
3. witness (　　)
4. strain (　　)
5. operations (　　)

a. assistance to those in need
b. the work involved in running a business
c. to stretch or force to the limit
d. kindness; spirit of giving
e. to see something take place

B **Fill in the blanks with appropriate expressions from the Vocabulary Check above. Change the word forms where necessary.**

1. Many politicians want to accept more immigrants although it would
   (   ) the system.
2. Thanks to the (   ) of the local community, all graduates will be receiving new iPads.
3. The police determined that there was only one person who (   )
   the robbery.
4. Maria is so well organized! We should put her in charge of (   ).
5. The earthquake victims were promised that (   ) would
   arrive soon.

News Story [2′ 33″]

D. Muir: Finally tonight here, "America Strong." The generosity—and it's needed. Americans helping their neighbors. Helping to put food on the table.

Tonight, the heroes across America feeding those in need. In Houston, dinner's almost ready. Sara Watson, a special education teacher, co-founding Feed the Front Line, to feed hospital workers, raising money, placing orders, ¹·_____

_____.

S. Watson, co-founder, Feed the Front Line: I've been making all the deliveries and it's the best part of my day, being able to go to a restaurant and know that this is helping them keep employees on their staff, and then go immediately to a hospital and see the people that these meals are gonna feed.

Health care workers: Thank you. Thank you.

D. Muir: Tonight, Sara ²·_____.

S. Watson: Hi, David.

D. Muir: Telling us, it's not just Houston. The idea is growing.

S. Watson: We're now in Houston, Dallas, Charlotte, Nashville, and Chicago, and we've served up over 5,000 meals this week.

D. Muir: In Centerville, Virginia, you'll remember Sal Speziale at Ciao Osteria, an Air Force veteran taking donations 3._____ _____. Now, they're taking donations to feed families, too.

S. Speziale, Ciao Osteria: Hi, David.

D. Muir: Telling us families are placing orders to help the hospital workers, but they also want to send food to families in need.

S. Speziale: They're basically ordering our food and saying, "Hey, 4. _____ _____?"

D. Muir: And Feeding America, the nation's largest hunger relief organization, tonight, listen to what they told us.

C. Babineaux-Fontenot, CEO, Feeding America: I've never witnessed the system being more strained than it is right now. Our estimations are that we will need to serve an additional 17.1 million people 5. _____.

D. Muir: Americans across this country answering the call.

Volunteer: Glad to be helping everybody in need right now.

D. Muir: Helping to put food on the table.

The Regional Food Bank of Oklahoma City. That's John in operations. And Lloyd Vine says, they are a determined few.

L. Vine: 6. _____, it's been myself and about eight other staff members.

D. Muir: As Americans across this country reach out to help their neighbors.

Resident 1: Thank God they're doing this.

Resident 2: This is really the only source of food we're getting at the moment.

D. Muir: And that is all you need to hear: Thank God they're doing this. So, we loved hearing from all of those volunteers across the country today. We're gonna stay on this. ⁷·_____. And so, if you're able, it's feedingamerica.org/feedthelove. I'm David Muir. I hope to see you right back here tomorrow. Good night.

5

Notes   **Houston**「ヒューストン〈テキサス州最大の都市。NASA（米国航空宇宙局）の施設があることでも有名〉」 **special education**「特別支援教育；特別ニーズ教育〈障がいの有無だけではなく，個々の子どもが持つ特別なニーズ（教育的支援の必要性）に応じた教育を提供しようという方針の教育〉」 **Feed the Front Line**「フィード・ザ・フロントライン〈医療機関など最前線で働く人々を支援する慈善組織〉」 **keep employees on their staff**「従業員の雇用維持」 **Dallas**「ダラス〈テキサス州北東部の都市〉」 **Charlotte**「シャーロット〈ノースカロライナ州最大の都市〉」 **Nashville**「ナッシュビル〈テネシー州の州都〉」 **Chicago**「シカゴ〈イリノイ州最大の都市〉」 **Centerville**「センタービル〈ワシントンD.C. の西方 20 マイルに位置するバージニア州の街〉」 **Ciao Osteria**「チャオ・オステリア」 **taking donations**「寄付を募っている」 **Feeding America**「フィーディング・アメリカ〈アメリカで最大のフードバンクネットワーク。国内の製造業者，小売業者，農家，企業，個人などからの寄付を通して食料や寄付金を調達し，全国のフードバンクに配布している〉」 **Regional Food Bank**「リージョナル・フードバンク〈オクラホマ州，オクラホマ・シティの NPO 法人〉」 **Oklahoma City**「オクラホマ・シティ〈オクラホマ州の州都〉」 **in operations**「運営している」 **determined few**「少数精鋭」 **As Americans across…**「〈なぜなら，アメリカ中で…〈直前の L. Vine さんのセリフとつながっている〉」 **Thank God**「感謝している；有り難い」

After   You Watch the News

Exercises

A Listen to the CD and fill in the blanks in the text.   ◎ CD 41

B Mark the following sentences true (T) or false (F) according to the information in the news story.

(   ) **1.** The co-founder of Feed the Front Line is a former teacher.

(   ) **2.** Hunger relief organizations are supplying food to hospital workers as well as needy families.

(   ) **3.** Sal Speziale is helping by collecting donations from Air Force veterans.

(   ) **4.** The system of volunteer feeding is expanding across the U.S.

(   ) **5.** According to one person, the need for relief is greater than ever before.

(   ) **6.** Some people claim that the only way they are able to eat is because of these volunteers.

C Translate the following Japanese into English. Then listen to the CD and practice the conversation with your partner.   ◎ CD 42

A: Lloyd called me this morning.

B: ¹. _____

_____?

A: No, this time they need help distributing the meals.

B: They never seem to have enough staff members. He must be so tired!

A: ². He is, but_____.

B: Hey—we should go help, too. ³. _____

_____. It's a real crisis.

A: I know. Actually, I already told Lloyd that we would both help. He's expecting us at 2:00.

B: Great!

1. 彼はまた食べ物のための寄付を集めているのですか。

2. 確かに、でもいつも元気なんだよ。

3. 今、困っている人がたくさんいるんだよ。

D Summary Practice: Fill in the blanks with suitable words beginning with the letters indicated. ◉ CD 43

ABC News reported on one uplifting aspect of the coronavirus
(¹· **c**   ): the (²· **g**   ) of Americans helping their
(³· **n**   ). From (⁴· **H**   ) to Dallas and
(⁵· **C**   ), (⁶· **v**   ) are finding ways to provide
(⁷· **r**   ) to those in need. Feed the (⁸· **F**   ) (⁹· **L**   ) is
bringing meals to (¹⁰· **h**   ) staff and at the same time, helping
(¹¹· **r**   ) to keep their (¹²· **e**   ). In
(¹³· **V**   ), Sal Speziale is collecting (¹⁴· **d**   ) to
feed needy (¹⁵· **f**   ) as well as hospital (¹⁶· **w**   ).
According to (¹⁷· **F**   ) (¹⁸· **A**   ), the largest
(¹⁹· **h**   ) (²⁰· **r**   ) organization in the country, over
(²¹· **s**   ) million additional people will be needing
(²²· **h**   ) throughout these difficult times. The recipients of the aid are
grateful to the volunteers across the country (²³· **r**   ) out to
help their neighbors.

E Discussion: Share your ideas and opinions with your classmates.

1. Find out about volunteer activities related to the coronavirus here in
Japan. What kind of special services are offered?

2. Have you or members of your family ever engaged in volunteer activities?
Explain what you have done. If you haven't, what kind of volunteer
activities might you be interested in?

　一般的に，平叙文のセンテンスの終わりではピッチは下降調で，話が「完結」した印象を与える。ところが，まだ話が続く場合は平叙文を接続詞 and で結ぶ。この場合，センテンスは重文となり，and の前でピッチを上げると「まだ話は続きますよ」という意図を伝えることができる。

　以下の例では，医療従事者に食事を届けるボランティアの仕事をしているサラ・ワトソンさんが，自身のボランティア活動の内容を and でつないで列挙している。この際，and 直前は，それぞれ上昇調（⤴）になっている。

— I've been making all the deliveries （⤴） and it's the best part of my
　　day, （⤴） being able to go to a restaurant （⤴） and know that
　　this is helping them keep employees on their staff, （⤴） and then
　　go immediately to a hospital （⤴） and see the people that these
　　meals are gonna feed. （⤵）　　　*(Volunteers Feeding Those in Need, p.83)*

　"I've been making all the deliveries （⤴） and..." の箇所を音声分析ソフト *Praat* で可視化すると以下のようにイントネーション曲線が deliveries の箇所で上昇しているのが分かる。なお，下図の上半分は音声波形（wave form），下半分はイントネーション曲線（intonation contour）を示している。

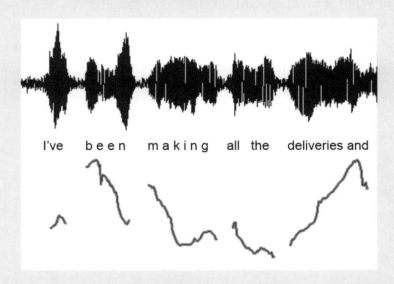

　また，以下の例では平叙文の文末ごとに上昇調が用いられている。これは，アメリカ英語のイントネーションの特徴のひとつになっている。

— This wood goes to local cattle ranchers, who build ah… fences around their area. (↗) And they're selling the stakes for those fences. (↗) And then it even shows right here how much money they're making. (↘)　　　　　　　　*(Amazon on the Brink, p.57)*

　さらに，次の例では，副詞句（for their livelihoods）の前の切れ目でもピッチは上昇調になっている。

— They rely on this business (↗) for their livelihoods, (↗) and I rely on them. (↘)　　　　　　　　*(Emergency Business Aid, p.62)*

Justice Department Turmoil

February 13

Air Date: February 16, 2020
Duration: 2′ 30″

Preview Questions

1. What kind of turmoil is currently being faced in the Department of Justice?

——現在，司法省はどのような混乱に直面しているのでしょうか。

2. How is Attorney General Barr responding to the accusations?

——バー司法長官は告発にどう対応していますか。

Warm-up Exercises

A Vocabulary Check: Choose the correct definition for each of the words below.

1. turmoil (　　)　　　　**a.** to quit or leave a job

2. confidante (　　)　　　**b.** shocking; scandalous

3. outrageous (　　)　　　**c.** turbulence; confusion

4. ally (　　)　　　　　　**d.** a person with whom one shares private matters

5. resign (　　)　　　　　**e.** a person who supports you or is on your side

B Fill in the blanks with appropriate expressions from the Vocabulary Check above. Change the word forms where necessary.

1. I always thought those two were real (   ), but recently, they don't seem to support each other.

2. That outfit is (   )! Go change your clothes before you go out.

3. If the real story becomes public, Jim might have to (   ).

4. There was a period of (   ) after two of the top bosses were transferred to another office.

5. The president's former (   ) wrote a shocking book full of inside gossip.

News Story [2′ 30″]

T. Llamas: Turmoil for the Department of Justice after Attorney General William Barr abruptly overruled his prosecutors in the case of longtime Trump confidante Roger Stone. Tonight, more than 1,100 former Justice Department officials are accusing Barr and the president of interfering, quote, "in the fair administration of justice." Here's ABC's Kyra Phillips.

5

K. Phillips: President Trump in Florida today, revvin' up the crowd as grand marshal at the Daytona 500. Taking a lap in his limo, the Beast, before thousands of NASCAR super fans. But tonight [1.] _____ _____ under attack by more than a thousand former Department of Justice officials, accusing them of interfering in, quote, "the fair administration of justice." Calling for William Barr to resign, saying it's "outrageous" the way he interfered in the case of convicted Trump ally Roger Stone. But in an exclusive interview with ABC News, Barr told Pierre Thomas he did not coordinate with the White House in the Stone case.

10

15

P. Thomas, ABC News: So, [2.] _____, did you talk to the president at all about your decision regarding the recommendations?

20

W. Barr, Attorney General: The recommendations on this case? Never.

P. Thomas: Anybody from the White House call you to try to influence you?

W. Barr: No, nope. I have… I have not discussed the Roger Stone case at the White House.

P. Thomas: At all?

W. Barr: At all.

K. Phillips: The president called the department's sentencing recommendation of [3.] _____ a "miscarriage of justice." It was thrown out, prompting all four prosecutors on the case to resign. The former DOJ employees and federal prosecutors accuse Barr of flouting principles based on an "evenhanded administration of justice," saying that the Stone case was [4.]_____.
Adding, "A person should not be given special treatment in a criminal prosecution because they are a close political ally of the president."

T. Llamas: And Kyra Phillips joins us now live from West Palm Beach, Florida, near the president's Mar-A-Lago resort, [5.] _____ _____. Kyra, many of these former Department of Justice officials have been critical of the administration in the past?

K. Phillips: You're absolutely right, Tom. These former employees served under Democratic and Republican presidents, and many of them [6.] _____ _____. As for Roger Stone, well, he's set to be sentenced on Thursday, Tom.

T. Llamas: Kyra Phillips for us tonight. Kyra, thank you.

Notes   **Department of Justice**「司法省〈= the United States Department of Justice（DOJ）〉」 **Attorney General**「司法長官」 **overruled his prosecutors**「検察の（厳しい）求刑を覆した〈ストーン被告に対して禁錮7～9年を求刑したが，これに対して，トランプ氏がツイッターで検察批判を展開した直後，司法省は求刑を軽減した〉」 **fair administration of justice**「公正な司法運営」 **revvin' up**「熱狂させる〈= revving up／rev up でエンジンの回転数を上げるという意味がある〉」 **grand marshal**「グランド・マーシャル〈パレードなどで（最も大きな喝采を浴びる）先頭車；先導役〉」 **Daytona 500**「デイトナ500カーレース〈自動車スピードレース大会 NASCAR カップ・シリーズの開幕戦で，2月の最終日曜日にフロリダ州のデイトナビーチ（Daytona Beach）で開催される〉」 **Taking a lap**「（レース場を）周回した」 **the Beast**「大統領専用車〈その重装備から the Beast と呼ばれている〉」 **NASCAR**「ナスカー〈= National Association for Stock Car Auto Racing〉」 **coordinate with ~**「～と（ストーン氏の量刑について）方針を調整する」 **sentencing recommendation**「（検事の）判決（量刑）意見」 **miscarriage of justice**「司法の誤審」 **thrown out**「却下された」 **flouting**「軽視している；逸脱している」 **evenhanded administration of justice**「公正な司法運営」 **A person should not be given ... because they are...**「〈文法的には a person に対して he or she と受けるところだが，性差別的にならないよう they が使われている〉」 **West Palm Beach**「ウェストパームビーチ〈フロリダ州南東部に位置する都市で，富裕層の別荘地〉」 **Mar-A-Lago resort**「マー・ア・ラーゴリゾート〈フロリダ州パームビーチにあるアメリカ合衆国国定歴史建造物でトランプ大統領の別荘。「マララーゴ」と音が連結して発音される〉」 **set to be sentenced**「判決（量刑）が下される予定」

Background of the News

トランプ大統領が司法への介入を強めている。連邦地裁は2020年2月20日，大統領選でトランプ陣営の選挙顧問だったロジャー・ストーン被告に対し，禁固3年4ヶ月を言い渡した。もともと7～9年の刑を求めていた検事の量刑意見（sentencing recommendation）を，トランプ大統領が「重すぎる」と批判し，その直後，司法省（Department of Justice）は，ストーン氏に対する求刑は「過度で正当な根拠がない」とする新たな裁判書類を提出して求刑を軽減する提言を出し，検事の意見を撤回させたため「司法介入」との批判が高まった。

トランプ大統領の盟友（confidante）のストーン氏は「ロシア疑惑」をめぐって，議会に偽証した罪などに問われていた。「ロシア疑惑」は，2016年大統領選でトランプ大統領の陣営がロシア政府と共謀し，民主党候補のヒラリー・クリントン元国務長官が不利になるよう工作したとされる疑惑のことである。

今回，米司法省の1,100人以上の元職員（former employees）らが，ウィリアム・バー司法長官（Attorney General William Barr）に辞任を求める書簡を公開した。トランプ大統領の求めに応じて，刑事裁判に介入（interfere）したとして「公正な司法運営」（fair administration of justice）を妨害したと批判したのである。

以前から，バー氏はトランプ大統領との親密さが指摘されており，中立性を疑う声が挙がっていた。元大統領補佐官のマイケル・フリン氏の裁判では，トランプ大統領に忖度する形で，司法省が起訴を突然取り下げる異例の判断をした。その時も，フリン氏の無罪を主張したトランプ氏の意向を踏まえて，バー氏が撤回した疑いが持たれていた。

Exercises

A Listen to the CD and fill in the blanks in the text.

CD 44

B Multiple Choice Questions

1. The former DOJ officials are expressing criticism because
   a. the president wants to put a political ally in the White House.
   b. the president and the attorney general have pardoned a criminal.
   c. the president and attorney general are interfering in a criminal case.

2. Which of the following statements about President Trump is *NOT* true?
   a. He admitted talking to Barr about the Roger Stone case.
   b. He disagreed with the original sentencing of Roger Stone.
   c. He spent the weekend at a resort and attended the Daytona 500.

3. William Barr
   a. claims the president influenced his action.
   b. has been asked to resign by former DOJ officials.
   c. firmly denied ever meeting Roger Stone at the White House.

4. The former DOJ officials who are making the complaints
   a. worked for both Democratic and Republican administrations.
   b. claim for the first time that the attorney general has been unfair.
   c. have unanimously overturned the decision made by the prosecutors.

C Translate the following Japanese into English. Then listen to the CD and practice the conversation with your partner. CD 45

A: Roger Stone is in the news again.

B: What did he do this time?

A: It's not what he did—¹· _____.

B: What did he do? Tell me!

A: ²· <u>Do you remember how</u> _____

_____?

B: Yeah. He called it a miscarriage of justice.

A: Well, now Barr has thrown out the recommendation and the four prosecutors have all quit!

B: What next? ³· _____

_____.

1. ウィリアム・バー氏がしたことです。

2. トランプ氏が，ストーン氏への判決勧告は厳しすぎると感じていたことを覚えていますか。

3. 大統領が自分の盟友を守るのはみんな知っています。

D Summary Practice: Fill in the blanks with suitable words beginning with the letters indicated. CD 46

The Department of Justice is facing (¹· t_____) as the
(²· A_____) (³· G_____) William Barr is accused of
(⁴· i_____) in the case of Trump (⁵· c_____)
Roger Stone. Over (⁶· o_____) (⁷· t_____) former DOJ officials
are calling for Barr to (⁸· r_____) after he (⁹· o_____)
the decision made by the (¹⁰· p_____) who work in his
department. The (¹¹· p_____), in (¹²· F_____) for the
(¹³· D_____) 500, felt that the (¹⁴· s_____) of (¹⁵· s_____)
to (¹⁶· n_____) years in prison was a "(¹⁷· m_____) of
(¹⁸· j_____)," and it was thrown out. This is not the first time former
officials have been (¹⁹· c_____) of interference by the Trump
(²⁰· a_____). This time, however, they are calling
Barr's actions "(²¹· o_____)," even though he firmly denies
any influence from the (²²· W_____) (²³· H_____).

E Discussion: Share your ideas and opinions with your classmates.

1. There are three branches of the United States government. What are they? What are their main responsibilities? What is meant by the expression "the system of checks and balances"?

2. Do an Internet search about Roger Stone. See what you can learn about his work and other activities. What was his relationship to Donald Trump? Find out what happened with his case in the end.

3. The news story suggests that this was not the only time that President Trump and Attorney General Barr were accused by former DOJ officials of interference in legal cases. Using the following key words, see what you can find out about another incident in June 2020:

   Geoffrey Berman   prosecutor   Southern District of New York

Appendix
巻末資料

Map of the Un

CANADA

Washington

Montana

North Dakota

Minnesota

Oregon

Idaho

South Dakota

Iow

Wyoming

Nevada

Nebraska

Utah

California

Colorado

Kansas

12

Oklahoma

19

Arizona

New Mexico

2

8   11

Texas

14

Alaska

MEXICO

Hawaii

ed States

❶〜㉑はニュースに登場した都市名で，州名はイタリックになっています。各都市の位置は，地図上に番号で示しています。

News Story 1
❶Palm Beach County, *Florida*
❷Plano, *Texas*
Michigan
❸Milwaukee, *Wisconsin*
❹New York, *New York*

News Story 3
❺Sanford, *North Carolina*
❻Raleigh, *North Carolina*

News Story 4 *West Virginia*

News Story 7
❼Middletown, *New Jersey*
❽Dallas, *Texas*

News Story 8 *California*
Minnesota

News Story 11
❾Atlanta, *Georgia*
❿Washington, D.C.
(the U.S. capital)

News Story 12
⓫Garland, *Texas*

News Story 13
⓬Los Angeles, *California*
❿Washington, D.C.
(the U.S. capital)
⓭Philadelphia, *Pennsylvania*

News Story 14
⓮Houston, *Texas*
❽Dallas, *Texas*
⓯Charlotte, *North Carolina*
⓰Nashville, *Tennessee*
⓱Chicago, *Illinois*
⓲Centerville, *Virginia*
⓳Oklahoma City, *Oklahoma*

News Story 15
⓴Daytona Beach, *Florida*
㉑West Palm Beach, *Florida*

99

TVニュース英語とは

1 アメリカ国内テレビニュース英語の特徴

　本書は直接ニューヨークで受信したテレビニュースから素材を選定し，米国 ABC 放送局本社からニュース映像を提供してもらいテキストに編集している。

　ニュース英語は伝えるメディア媒体の種類上，大きく分けて３種類に分類される。第１は新聞，雑誌などに代表される活字で伝えられるもの，第２にはラジオのように音声情報に頼る媒体から提供されるもの，そして第３番目はネットやテレビを介して音声情報と画像情報が同時に供給されるニュースである。ここでは，第３番目のメディア媒体であるテレビ放送におけるニュース英語の特徴を簡単にまとめてみた。ニュース英語というと使用される英語もフォーマルなイメージがあるが，実際には以下で述べるように口語的な特徴も多く見られる。ここで引用している例文は最近の *ABC World News Tonight* で実際使われたものばかりである。

1.1 ニュースの構成

　まず，放送スタジオにいるアンカーパーソンが，そのニュースの中心情報をリード部分で述べ，何についてのニュースであるかを視聴者に知らせる。アンカーパーソンは，ごく短くそのニュースの概要を紹介し，リポーターへとバトンタッチする。次にリポーターが現地からのリポートを，時にはインタビュー等を交えながら詳しく報告する，というのがテレビニュースの一般的なパターンになっている。それを略図で示したのが次の図である。ひとつのニュースの放送時間は割合短く，普通 1.5 〜 3 分程である。

●ニュースの構成

Anchor, Anchorperson

LEAD
INTRODUCTION（放送スタジオ）

リポーターへの導入表現

MAIN BODY（現地からのリポート，
　　　　　　　　インタビューなど）

リポーターの結びの表現

Reporter

1.2 比較的速いスピード

　発話速度はセンター入試のリスニング問題で平均毎分約 155 ～ 160 語，英検 2 級では 150 語前後ぐらいだと言われている。しかし，生の（authentic）英語になると，かなり発話速度が速くなる。英語母語話者が話す速度は，インフォーマルな会話の場合，平均毎分 210 語で，速い場合は人によって 230 wpm (words per minute) になる。典型的なフォーマル・スタイルの英語である，アメリカ国内のテレビニュース放送（ABC 放送）を筆者が調べたところ，発話速度は平均 163 ～ 198 wpm であることが分かった。生の英語でも一般的にフォーマルな話しことばほど発話速度は落ちてくるが，アメリカ国内用のテレビニュースは比較的速い方に分類される。

1.3 不完全文の多用

　テレビニュース英語では，be 動詞や主語，動詞が省略された「不完全文」が多く，端的で箇条書き的な表現が好んで使われる。例えば，以下の例は ABC 放送で実際に使用されていた文である。これらは散列文（loose sentence）として，書きことばでは非文とされるが，テレビニュース英語ではよく現れる不完全文の一例と考えられる。

— Tonight, fears the U.S. is on the brink of an outbreak among the birds.

　上記を補足的に書き換えると以下のようになる。
— Tonight, [there are] fears [that] the U.S. is on the brink of an outbreak [of bird flu] among the birds.

　次は，シェイクスピアが人気があることを伝えるニュースからの例である。
— Four hundred years, 20 generations and still going strong.

　これを，説明的に補足すれば，以下のようになる。
— Four hundred years [or] 20 generations [have passed since he died and he is] still going strong.

　新聞英語の見出しでは be 動詞が省略されることはよく知られているが，テレビニュース英語では，主語・一般動詞・be 動詞・関係代名詞などを省略し，箇条書き的な文体で情報を生き生きと伝える。文法より，伝達する意味内容を重視するため，短い語句をたたみかけるように次々つなぐのである。特に，ニュースの冒頭部分で何についての報道であるか，そのトピックを告げるときにこの文体はよく用いられる。以下の（∧）は，そこに何らかの項目が省略されていることを示している。

— ∧ Sixty-nine years old, ∧ married for 35 years, ∧ lives in Honolulu.
— The weather was calm, the tide ∧ high, ...
— This is the fifth anniversary of the Columbine tragedy, ∧ the worst school shooting in U.S. history.
— Today, ∧ the battle for Ohio.

このような不完全文を使うことによって，ニュースに緊張感や臨場感を持たせ，視聴者の興味を引き付けている。テレビニュースの場合は視聴者の視覚に訴える画像情報があるので，完全で説明的な文体を使用するよりは，むしろ箇条書的な不完全文の方が視聴者にアピールしやすい。

1.4 現在時制が多い

最新のニュースを伝えるというテレビニュースの即時性を考えれば，現在形や近い未来を表す表現が多いことは容易に予想される。米 ABC 放送のニュースにおける時制について調べたところ，現在形と現在進行形で 46% を占めていることが分かった。現在形や進行形の多用は臨場感を生み出す。

— The world's largest carmakers say they *are going to* lower the frame on sport utility vehicles...
— ..., and Rome's police *are* aggressively *enforcing* the new law, ...
— Americans now *spend* more time on the job than workers in any other developed country.
— ...their budget shortfalls *are* so severe they *are going* to raise taxes.
— Now AmeriCorps *is telling* future volunteers there may be no place for them.

新聞などの書きことばにおけるニュース英語では，未来を表すのに "be expected to", "be scheduled to", "be to" などやや固い表現がよく使われるが，口語的なニュース英語では "will" が好んで使用される。

— In this crowd, there are damning claims that she is being starved, that she *will* suffer.
— For now, some colleges *will* ignore scores for the new writing section, ...

1.5 伝達動詞は say が多い

ニュース英語の特徴として「誰々がこう言った，何々によればこういうことである」といった構文が多く現れる。主語＋伝達動詞＋（that）節という構文では，伝達動詞は say が圧倒的に多く用いられる。構文に変化を付けるために，主節が文中に挿入されたり、文尾に後置されたりする場合も多い。

— One result of higher temperatures, *says* the government, is more extremes in the weather, ...
— But that's the male reaction, *say* the researchers.

直接話法では，Mary said to Cathy, "I like your new car." というように，「発言者＋伝達動詞」が被伝達部に先行するのが一般的である。ニュースの英語では，このような直接話法を使って「…が〜と言いました」という表現はよく見られるが，以下のように「発言者＋伝達動詞」が被伝達部の後に出てくる場合も多い。また，以下の冒頭例のように，発言

者が人称代名詞以外の名詞であれば，伝達動詞が先に来る。

— "It turns out they're a lot more like people than we thought," *says* the director of the Wolong reserve.
— "I'm going to use an expression," he *says*.
— "It's strange to be here," he *says*.
— "Soon, we're planning to fly from Baghdad to Europe," he *says*.

1.6 縮約形の多用

　以下のような指示代名詞，人称代名詞や疑問代名詞の後の be 動詞，助動詞の縮約形（contraction）がよく使われる：it's, that's, we'll, don't, I'm, you're, here's, they're, we're, we've, can't, won't, what's.

　縮約形はくだけた会話英語の特徴である。以下の例からも分かるように，テレビニュース英語では新聞英語とは異なって，縮約形の使用によりインフォーマルな雰囲気が出ている。書きことばの原稿をただ読み上げるのではなくて，視聴者にとって親しみやすい響きを与える口語的なスタイルが心がけられている。

— And the reason why, George, is *they've* learned that the Made in the USA tag carries real weight in China.
— *It's* been decades since then, but polio is still very much alive.
— Add it all up and America's happiest person *isn't* Tom Selleck, *it's* Alvin Wong.
— ..., the one that comes when you *can't* put down the Blackberry or iPhone at home, ...
— *She's* constantly juggling his needs and those of the Cincinnati ad agency she works for.

2 テレビニュースの表現

2.1 冒頭部分の特徴

　ストーリーの全体を予想させたり，ニュース内容に期待を持たせたりするために，ニュースの冒頭には短いインパクトのある表現や，やや大げさな表現が置かれる。以下の例は気球に乗って初めて世界一周に成功した人のニュースである。

— *History was made today* above the Sahara Desert — man, for the first time, has flown around the world nonstop in a balloon.

　新聞英語では，冒頭の文（lead）で読者の注意をひきつけるために，書き方が工夫されることが多い。テレビニュース英語でも，新しいニュースの始まりの部分では疑問文，繰り返し，文法的に不完全な文などを用いて視聴者の興味をひきつけようとする。

— Finally this evening, ***not just another pretty face***.
— ***The weather, the weather, always the weather.***
— Finally, this evening, ***will they turn the panda cam back on again?***

2.2 リポーター紹介の表現

　アンカーパーソンがニュースの主要情報を紹介した後，リポーターにバトンタッチする時の表現である。日本語のニュースでは「では，現場の〜がリポートします」に当たる部分で，次のように様々なバリエーションがある。

— And tonight, Dr. Richard Besser takes us to a remote part of the world, ...
— ABC's Abbie Boudreau is in Provo, Utah.
— It's a duel in the Capitol Hill cafeteria and Jon Karl explains.
— We asked Bianna Golodryga to find out.
— Lisa Stark explains why.
— Here's John Berman on health, wealth and birth order.
— Jim Avila is at a McDonald's in Newark, New Jersey, tonight. Jim?

　アンカーパーソンが，現場のリポーターや別の放送スタジオにいるニューズキャスターを呼び出す時には，その人にファーストネームで呼びかける。呼びかけられた人は，自分の読む原稿が終了して元のアンカーパーソンに戻したい時にもまたファーストネームで呼びかける。名前の呼び合いがバトンタッチの合図にもなっている。

— **D. Sawyer:** Jim Avila is at a McDonald's in Newark, New Jersey, tonight. ***Jim?***
— **J. Avila:** Well, ***Diane***, in this one McDonald's alone, more than 1,000 people applied for what's likely to be four jobs.
— **J. Karl:** ..., it's probably going to last in a landfill somewhere for thousands and thousands of years. ***Diane?***
— **D. Sawyer:** Okay, ***Jon***. That was one sad spoon earlier.

2.3 リポーターの結びの表現

　リポーターは現場からの報道の最後を決まりきった表現で結ぶ。リポーターの名前，放送局，リポート地が告げられる。それぞれの間にポーズを入れ，すこしゆっくり目に言われるのが共通した特徴である。

— John Berman, ABC News, New York.
— Lisa Stark, ABC News, Washington.
— Barbara Pinto, ABC News, Chicago.
— Jeffrey Kofman, ABC News, Nairobi.

2.4 ニュースとニュースのつなぎ表現

ひとつのニュースから別のニュースに移行する時，何らかのシグナルがある方が視聴者としても分かりやすい。後続のニュース内容に応じた様々な表現を使って新しいニュースの始まりを合図している。

— *And finally tonight,* what makes someone the happiest person in America?

— *Now to a story about* the struggle between technology and family time.

— *And finally,* our "Person of the Week."

— *And now, we move on to* an incredible scene across the country today beneath the iconic symbol of corporate America, McDonald's.

— *Tonight,* we want to tell you about something new in the use of brain surgery to control tremors from a number of causes.

2.5 コマーシャル前のつなぎの表現

コマーシャルの間にチャンネルを変えられないよう，次のニュースの予告をする際，以下のような様々な工夫した表現が使われる。

— And when we come back, a master class in enduring crisis from the Japanese people.

— And coming up next, what's become one of those annual rites of spring.

— When we come back here on the broadcast tonight, we switch gears and take a look at this.

2.6 番組終了時の表現

その日のニュース番組は，挨拶や次回の予告などで終わる。

— And be sure to watch "Nightline" later on tonight. Our co-anchor Bill Weir is here — right here in Japan, as well.

— And we'll see you back here from Japan tomorrow night. Until then we hope you have a good night at home in the United States.

— And that's it from us for now.

最近のニュースに現れた略語

▼A

AAA [Automobile Association of America] 全米自動車連盟

AARP [American Association of Retired Persons] 全米退職者協会

ABA [American Bar Association] 米国弁護士協会

ABC [American Broadcasting Companies] ABC放送

ABC [American-born Chinese] アメリカ生まれの中国人

ACA [Affordable Care Act] 医療費負担適正化法

ACLU [American Civil Liberties Union] 米国自由人権協会

ACT [American College Test] 米大学入学学力テスト

ADHD [attention-deficit hyperactivity disorder] 注意欠陥・多動性障害

AI [artificial intelligence] 人工知能

AIDS [acquired immune deficiency syndrome] 後天性免疫不全症候群

AMA [American Medical Association] 米国医師会

ANC [African National Congress] アフリカ民族会議

AOL [America Online] アメリカ・オンライン：アメリカのパソコン通信大手

AP [Associated Press] AP通信社：アメリカ最大の通信社

ASEAN [Association of Southeast Asian Nations] アセアン；東南アジア諸国連合

ATF [Federal Bureau of Alcohol, Tobacco and Firearms] アルコール・たばこ・火器局 [米]

ATM [automated teller (telling) machine] 現金自動預け払い機

AT&T [American Telephone and Telegraph Corporation] 米国電話電信会社

ATV [all-terrain vehicle] オフロードカー

▼B

BART [Bay Area Rapid Transit] バート：サンフランシスコ市の通勤用高速鉄道

BBC [British Broadcasting Corporation] 英国放送協会

BYU [Brigham Young University] ブリガム・ヤング大学

▼C

CBO [Congressional Budget Office] 連邦議会予算局

CBS [Columbia Broadcasting System] （米国）コロンビア放送会社

CCTV [China Central Television] 国営中国中央テレビ

CDC [Centers for Disease Control and Prevention] 疾病対策センター [米]

CEO [chief executive officer] 最高経営役員

CHP [Department of California Highway Patrol] カリフォルニア・ハイウェイ・パトロール

CIA [Central Intelligence Agency] 中央情報局 [米]

CNN [Cable News Network] シー・エヌ・エヌ

COLA   [cost-of-living adjustment] 生活費調整
COO   [chief operating officer] 最高執行責任者
COVID-19   [coronavirus disease 2019] 新型コロナウイルス感染症
CPSC   [(U.S.) Consumer Product Safety Commission] 米消費者製品安全委員会
CT   [computerized tomography] CTスキャン；コンピュータ断層撮影

▼D

DC   [District of Columbia] コロンビア特別区
DHS   [Department of Homeland Security] 国土安全保障省［米］
DJIA   [Dow Jones Industrial Average] ダウ（ジョーンズ）工業株30種平均
DMV   [Department of Motor Vehicles] 自動車局：車両登録や運転免許を扱う
DMZ   [Demilitarized Zone] 非武装地帯
DNA   [deoxyribonucleic acid] デオキシリボ核酸：遺伝子の本体
DNC   [Democratic National Committee] 民主党全国委員会
DOD   [Department of Defense] アメリカ国防総省
DOJ   [Department of Justice] 司法省［米］
DPRK   [Democratic People's Republic of Korea] 朝鮮民主主義人民共和国
DST   [Daylight Saving Time] サマータイム；夏時間
DVD   [digital versatile disc] ディーブイディー：大容量光ディスクの規格
DWI   [driving while intoxicated] 酒酔い運転；酒気帯び運転

▼E

EDT   [Eastern Daylight (saving) Time] 東部夏時間［米］
EMS   [European Monetary System] 欧州通貨制度
EPA   [Environmental Protection Agency] 環境保護庁［米］
ER   [emergency room] 救急処置室
ES cell [embryonic stem cell] ES細胞；胚性幹細胞：あらゆる種類の組織・臓器に分化
             できる細胞
EU   [European Union] 欧州連合
EV   [electric(al) vehicle] 電気自動車

▼F

FAA   [Federal Aviation Administration] 連邦航空局［米］
FBI   [Federal Bureau of Investigation] 連邦捜査局［米］
FCC   [Federal Communications Commission] 連邦通信委員会［米］
FDA   [Food and Drug Administration] 食品医薬品局［米］
FEMA   [Federal Emergency Management Agency] 連邦緊急事態管理局［米］
FIFA   [Federation of International Football Associations (Fédération Internationale de
             Football Association)] フィーファ；国際サッカー連盟
FRB   [Federal Reserve Bank] 連邦準備銀行［米］
FRB   [Federal Reserve Board] 連邦準備制度理事会［米］

FTC [Federal Trade Commission] 連邦取引委員会［米］

FWS [Fish and Wildlife Service] 魚類野生生物局［米］

▼G

G8 [the Group of Eight] 先進（主要）8 カ国（首脳会議）

G-20 [the Group of Twenty (Finance Ministers and Central Bank Governors)] 主要20 カ国・地域財務相・中央銀行総裁会議

GAO [General Accounting Office] 会計検査院［米］

GDP [gross domestic product] 国内総生産

GE [General Electric Company] ゼネラル・エレクトリック：アメリカの大手総合電機メーカー

GM [General Motors Corporation] ゼネラル・モーターズ社：アメリカの大手自動車メーカー

GMA [Good Morning America] グッド・モーニング・アメリカ〈ABC放送の朝の情報・ニュース番組〉

GMT [Greenwich Mean Time] グリニッジ標準時

GNP [gross national product] 国民総生産

GOP [Grand Old Party] ゴップ：アメリカ共和党の異名

GPA [grade point average] 成績平均点

GPS [global positioning system] 全地球測位システム

▼H

HBO [Home Box Office] ホーム・ボックス・オフィス：アメリカ最大手のペイケーブル番組供給業者

HHS [Department of Health and Human Services] 保健社会福祉省［米］

HIV [human immunodeficiency virus] ヒト免疫不全ウイルス

HMO [Health Maintenance Organization] 保健維持機構［米］

HMS [Her (His) Majesty's Ship] 英国海軍；英国海軍艦船

HRW [Human Rights Watch] ヒューマン・ライツ・ウォッチ

HSBC [Hongkong and Shanghai Banking Corporation Limited] 香港上海銀行

▼I

IBM [International Business Machines Corporation] アイ・ビー・エム

ICBM [intercontinental ballistic missile] 大陸間弾道ミサイル（弾）

ICE [Immigration and Customs Enforcement] 移民税関捜査局［米］

ID [identification] 身分証明書

IDF [Israel Defense Forces] イスラエル国防軍

IMF [International Monetary Fund] 国際通貨基金

Inc. [~ Incorporated] ～会社；会社組織の；有限会社

INS [Immigration and Naturalization Service] 米国移民帰化局

IOC [International Olympic Committee] 国際オリンピック委員会

IPCC [Intergovernmental Panel on Climate Change] 気候変動に関する政府間パネル

IQ [intelligence quotient] 知能指数

IRA [Irish Republican Army] アイルランド共和軍

IRS [Internal Revenue Service] 内国歳入庁［米］

ISIS [Islamic State of Iraq and Syria] イスラム国

IT [information technology] 情報テクノロジー；情報技術

IUCN [International Union for Conservation of Nature (and Natural Resources)] 国際自然保護連合

▼J

JCAHO [Joint Commission on Accreditation of Healthcare Organizations] 医療施設認定合同審査会［米］

JFK [John Fitzgerald Kennedy] ケネディー：アメリカ第35代大統領

▼L

LA [Los Angeles] ロサンゼルス

LED [light-emitting diode] 発光ダイオード

LLC [limited liability company] 有限責任会社

LNG [liquefied natural gas] 液化天然ガス

▼M

M&A [merger and acquisition] 企業の合併・買収

MADD [Mothers Against Drunk Driving] 酒酔い運転に反対する母親の会［米］

MERS [Middle East Respiratory Syndrome (coronavirus)] マーズコロナウイルス

MLB [Major League Baseball] メジャー・リーグ・ベースボール［米］

MMR [measles-mumps-rubella vaccine] MMRワクチン：はしか，おたふく風邪，風疹の３種混合の予防接種

MRI [magnetic resonance imaging] 磁気共鳴映像法

MVP [most valuable player] 最高殊勲選手；最優秀選手

▼N

NAFTA [North Atlantic Free Trade Area] ナフタ；北大西洋自由貿易地域

NASA [National Aeronautics and Space Administration] ナサ；航空宇宙局［米］

NASCAR [National Association for Stock Car Auto Racing] 全米自動車競争協会

NASDAQ [National Association of Securities Dealers Automated Quotations]（証券）ナスダックシステム；相場情報システム［米］

NATO [North Atlantic Treaty Organization] 北大西洋条約機構

NBA [National Basketball Association] 全米バスケットボール協会

NBC [National Broadcasting Company] NBC放送

NCAA [National Collegiate Athletic Association] 全米大学体育協会

NCIC [National Crime Information Center] 全米犯罪情報センター

NFL	[National Football League] ナショナル［米プロ］・フットボール・リーグ
NGO	[non-governmental organization] 非政府（間）組織；民間非営利団体
NHL	[National Hockey League] 北米プロアイスホッケー・リーグ
NHTSA	[National Highway Traffic Safety Administration] 幹線道路交通安全局［米］
NIH	[National Institutes of Health] 国立保健研究［米］
NRA	[National Rifle Association] 全米ライフル協会
NSA	[National Security Agency] 国家安全保障局［米］
NTSA	[National Technical Services Association] 全国輸送安全委員会［米］
NTSB	[National Transportation Safety Board] 国家運輸安全委員会［米］
NV	[Nevada] ネバダ州（アメリカ）
NYPD	[New York City Police Department] ニューヨーク市警察

▼O

OMB	[the Office of Management and Budget] 行政管理予算局
OPEC	[Organization of Petroleum Exporting Countries] 石油輸出国機構

▼P

PGA	[Professional Golfers' Association] プロゴルフ協会〈正式には，全米プロゴルフ協会はProfessional Golfers' Association of America（PGA of America）〉
PGD	[pre-implantation genetic diagnosis] 着床前遺伝子診断
PIN	[personal identification number] 暗証番号；個人識別番号
PLO	[Palestine Liberation Organization] パレスチナ解放機構
POW	[prisoner of war] 戦争捕虜
PVC	[polyvinyl chloride] ポリ塩化ビニル

▼Q

QB	[quarterback] クォーターバック（アメリカン・フットボール）

▼R

RAF	[Royal Air Force] 英国空軍
RNC	[Republican National Committee] 共和党全国委員会
ROK	[Republic of Korea] 大韓民国
ROTC	[Reserve Officers' Training Corps] 予備役将校訓練団［米］
RV	[recreational vehicle] リクリエーション用自動車

▼S

SAM	[surface-to-air missile] 地対空ミサイル
SARS	[Severe Acute Respiratory Syndrome] 重症急性呼吸器症候群
SAT	[Scholastic Aptitude Test] 大学進学適性試験［米］
SEC	[(U.S.) Securities and Exchange Commission] 米証券取引委員会
SNS	[social networking service] ソーシャル・ネットワーキング・サービス：インタ

ーネットを介して，友人や知人の輪を広げていくためのオンラインサービス

START [Strategic Arms Reduction Treaty] 戦略兵器削減条約

STD [sexually transmitted (transmissible) diseases] 性感染症

SUV [sport-utility vehicle] スポーツ・ユーティリティ・ビークル；スポーツ汎用車

SWAT [Special Weapons and Tactics] スワット；特別機動隊 [米]

▼T

TB [tuberculosis] 結核

TOB [takeover bid] 株式の公開買付制度：企業の支配権を得るためにその企業の株式を買い集めること

TPP [Trans-Pacific Partnership] 環太平洋戦略的経済連携協定

TSA [Transportation Security Administration] 運輸保安局 [米]

▼U

UA [United Airlines] ユナイテッド航空

UAE [United Arab Emirates] アラブ首長国連邦

UAW [United Automobile Workers] 全米自動車労働組合

UCLA [University of California at Los Angeles] カリフォルニア大学ロサンゼルス校

UK [United Kingdom (of Great Britain and Northern Ireland)] 英国；グレートブリテンおよび北部アイルランド連合王国：英国の正式名

UN [United Nations] 国際連合

UNICEF [United Nations International Children's Emergency Fund] ユニセフ；国連児童基金 〈現在の名称はUnited Nations Children's Fund〉

USAF [United States Air Force] 米空軍

USC [the University of Southern California] 南カリフォルニア大学

USDA [United States Department of Agriculture] 米農務省

USGS [United States Geological Survey] 米国地質調査所

USMC [United States Marine Corps] 米国海兵隊

このテキストのメインページ
www.kinsei-do.co.jp/plusmedia/411
次のページの QR コードを読み取ると
直接ページにジャンプできます

オンライン映像配信サービス「plus⁺Media」について

本テキストの映像は plus⁺Media ページ（www.kinsei-do.co.jp/plusmedia）から、ストリーミング再生でご利用いただけます。手順は以下に従ってください。

ログイン

●ご利用には、ログインが必要です。
サイトのログインページ（www.kinsei-do.co.jp/plusmedia/login）へ行き、plus⁺Media パスワード（次のページのシールをはがしたあとに印字されている数字とアルファベット）を入力します。

●パスワードは各テキストにつき1つです。
有効期限は、<u>はじめてログインした時点から1年間</u>になります。

ログインページ

[利用方法]

次のページにある QR コード、もしくは plus⁺Media トップページ（www.kinsei-do.co.jp/plusmedia）から該当するテキストを選んで、そのテキストのメインページにジャンプしてください。

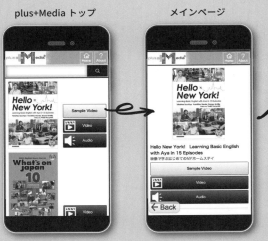

plus+Media トップ　　メインページ　　メニューページ　　再生画面

「Video」「Audio」をタッチすると、それぞれのメニューページにジャンプしますので、そこから該当する項目を選べば、ストリーミングが開始されます。

[推奨環境]

iOS (iPhone, iPad)	OS: iOS 6 〜 13 ブラウザ：標準ブラウザ	Android	OS: Android 4.x 〜 10.0 ブラウザ：標準ブラウザ、Chrome
PC	OS: Windows 7/8/8.1/10, MacOS X　ブラウザ: Internet Explorer 10/11, Microsoft Edge, Firefox 48以降, Chrome 53以降, Safari		

※最新の推奨環境についてはウェブサイトをご確認ください。
※上記の推奨環境を満たしている場合でも、機種によってはご利用いただけない場合もあります。また、推奨環境は技術動向等により変更される場合があります。予めご了承ください。

このシールをはがすと
plus+Media 利用のための
パスワードが
記載されています。

一度はがすと元に戻すことは
できませんのでご注意下さい。

◀ここからはがして下さい

4115 BROADCAST
(ABC) 3   plus+Media

本書には CD（別売）があります

Broadcast: ABC WORLD NEWS TONIGHT 3
映像で学ぶ ABCワールドニュース 3

2021年1月20日　初版第1刷発行
2022年8月31日　初版第4刷発行

編著者　　山　根　　繁
　　　　　Kathleen Yamane

発行者　　福　岡　正　人
発行所　　株式会社　金　星　堂

（〒101-0051）東京都千代田区神田神保町 3-21
Tel. (03) 3263-3828（営業部）
　　(03) 3263-3997（編集部）
Fax (03) 3263-0716
http://www.kinsei-do.co.jp

編集担当　松本明子・西田 碧　　　　　Printed in Japan
印刷所・製本所／大日本印刷株式会社

ISBN978-4-7647-4115-7 C1082